Revolution Anyone?
TROTSKY IN CANADA, 1917

M. RAOUL BOYER

Yesterday Today Publishing
Dieppe, New Brunswick
Canada
yesterdaytoday5555@gmail.com

Copyright © 2021 by M. Raoul Boyer

All rights reserved. No part of this book may be reproduced or transmitted in any form or by any means, electronic or mechanical, including photocopying, or by any information storage or retrieval system, without permission in writing from the publisher.

ISBN 978-0-9918558-2-7 (paperback)
ISBN 978-0-9918558-3-4 (ebook)

Yesterday Today Publishing,
Dieppe, New Brunswick
Canada
yesterdaytoday5555@gmail.com

Cover and interior design by Tara Mayberry, TeaBerry Creative

CONTENTS

Introduction 1
Beginnings 5
New York, 1917 11
44 Whitehall Avenue, New York 23
Russian Revolution 31
Halifax, Nova Scotia, Canada 55
Amherst, Nova Scotia 69
"Irreproachable Russian Revolutionaries" 73
New York 77
Letting the World Know 79
Settling In 89
Friction 93
Tornio, Finland 99
Natalya Sedova 103
Pressure Increases 107
Bibliography 119

INTRODUCTION

"An undersized, wild-eyed, fanatic little plucked-bantam of a Russian expatriate literally set out from Hoboken to upset the provisional government of Russia, prevent the formation of a republic, stop the war with Germany and prevent interference from other governments—that was his open boast. And, if such a mission can be crowned with success, he succeeded."

—Inspector Thomas Tunney, head of the NYPD's anti-terrorist unit called the "Bomb Squad," 1918

How did Leon Trotsky, one of the twentieth century's most passionate and dangerous communists, become imprisoned for a month in an internment camp in Amherst, Nova Scotia, Canada? How did one of the most influential leaders of the Russian Revolution—its greatest orator, who would single-handedly create the Soviet Red Army—find himself confined with eight hundred and fifty German prisoners of war during World War I? How did the man who would influence the creation of the fledgling Soviet nation end up being carried off a ship in Halifax Harbour, screaming, while his fellow passengers (most of whom were revolutionaries as well), and his wife and children watched? How did this socialist revolutionary become imprisoned in Canada on his way home to join the revolution that had started in his absence?

This is a story of espionage, conspiracy, and counter-conspiracy. It is the saga of a German-American Jewish banker's efforts to finance the overthrow of Russian Czar Nicholas II because of his ethnic cleansing of Jews in Russia. It is a saga of agents and double agents, including the supposed "Ace of Spies" Sidney Reilly, whose self-interest and subterfuge ultimately caused his own death by firing squad in Russia in 1925. Intermingle this with the attempt to strike a deal with the antisemitic American car manufacturer Henry Ford to provide vehicles to Russia (Ford would eventually build and sell cars in Stalin's Russia in the late 1920s). We will examine Reilly's connection to the explosion of a large munitions plant belonging to the company that also leased the buildings that housed German P.O.W.s in Amherst, Nova Scotia. This is also the same facility that hosted Leon Trotsky less than three months later.

Was Trotsky's detention a warranted act designed to protect the Allied cause from a man hell-bent on removing Russia from the war, thus creating a one-front conflict? Or was it an attempt to force Trotsky into becoming a British agent by incarcerating him until he accepted? Could it have been that, after accepting money to further the communist cause, Trotsky was put on ice in order to give him a more legitimate cover story?

We will also look at the conditions under which Trotsky and his fellow revolutionaries existed in Amherst. We will examine all facets of his stay, including his interactions with the camp commander, the guards, and of course, his fellow detainees. Also, we will look at the visitors Trotsky may have had while in Amherst. This included Claude Dansey, MI5's head of port intelligence. Dansey is credited with giving the final command to release Trotsky from Amherst. Henry Ford, or someone representing him, may have also ventured to Amherst to speak with the man about securing the Russian market for his cars, trucks, and tractors. Even though Leon Trotsky's real name was Lev Bronstein, Henry Ford was never one to let his antisemitic feelings get in the way of profit.

Leon Trotsky was undoubtedly one of the most polarizing figures of the early twentieth century. Never one to stand for half-measures, he often set events in motion by the strength of his fiery will. This is never more evident than in the story that we are about to tell.

Leon Trotsky (Wikimedia Commons)

BEGINNINGS

Lev Davidovich Bronstein was born on 26 October 1879 in Yanovka, in the Kherson Province in New Russia, which is now part of southern Ukraine. He was the fifth child of eight belonging to prosperous Jewish farmers David and Aneta Bronstein. While not religious, the Bronsteins prospered in an area of Russia not immune to the anti-Jewish pogroms rampant at the time. They benefited from the economic expansionism of the late nineteenth century and from the world's hunger for Russian wheat. Their proximity to railways and to the Black Sea helped them to prosper as well.

Trotsky received his education in the Black Sea port city of Odessa. From 1888 until 1895 he was educated based on the German *Gymnasium* model, which was a type of secondary school which placed greater emphasis on academic learning. This educational model better reflected the international cosmopolitan make-up of the city at that time. Odessa's architecture, education, literature, and overall intellectual internationalism heavily influenced the young Trotsky. The city's population, unlike much of the Russian Empire at the time, was drawn heavily from those who hailed from different parts of the globe. Italians, English, Armenians, Persians, Germans, Georgians, Arabs, Greeks, and French nationals all cohabitated the city. Odessa also contained a large working class receptive to radical political ideas and organizations. All these factors would combine to help create a man international in his outlook and radical in his politics.

In 1898, Trotsky was imprisoned for two years for writing, printing, and distributing Marxist revolutionary pamphlets. This was dangerous in the years after the revolutionary Narodnaya Volya (The People's Will) assassinated Czar Alexander II in 1881. While in the prison in Moscow, in the summer of 1899, Trotsky married Aleksandra Sokolovskaya (1872–1938), a fellow Marxist. The wedding ceremony was performed by a Jewish chaplain. In 1900, Trotsky was then again arrested and sentenced to four years of exile in Siberia after his two-year incarceration was completed. He was permitted to be joined by his wife in exile. They had two daughters, Zinaida (1901 – 5 January 1933) and Nina (1902 – 9 June 1928), both born in Siberia.

In 1902, at the urging of his wife, Trotsky escaped from Siberia hidden in the back of a hay wagon. His wife and two daughters would leave later, yet Trotsky, who had assumed the name of his Odessan jailer, would never reunite with his family again. He would divorce his wife shortly afterward and then send his children to be raised by his parents in Yanovka. Trotsky left Russia to live in London, where he met and worked with Vladimir Lenin at a newspaper named *Iskra*. London was also where, in 1902, Trotsky met his second wife, Natalya Sedova. They married in 1903.

The Russian revolutionaries living in London at the time were split between the new and the old, or more specifically, between the Menshevik and the Bolshevik factions. Most of the editors and writers at *Iskra* joined the Russian Social Democratic Labour Party (RSDLP). At the second congress, held in London in 1903, there was a dispute between Lenin and Julius Martov, a compatriot and fellow editor. Martov wanted an all-inclusive democratic party that allowed workers' voices to be heard. Lenin had wanted a party, conversely, which ruled from the top with an iron hand and allowed for little input from workers and the proletariat.

Trotsky predicted at the time that "Lenin's methods lead to this: the party organization substitutes itself for the party, the central committee…The party must seek a guarantee of its stability in its own base, in an active and self-reliant proletariat, and not in its top caucus…which the revolution may suddenly swing away with its wing."

After much debate and in-fighting between Bolsheviks and Mensheviks, Lenin, who supported the former, and Trotsky, who supported the latter, had a falling out, which lasted until 1917. That decision would resurface and haunt Trotsky after Lenin's death.

Trotsky spent most of the period between 1903 and 1917 attempting to unify the various socialist factions. At the outbreak of World War I, Trotsky was in Vienna but was forced to flee to Switzerland to avoid incarceration for being a Russian émigré. During his time in Switzerland, he wrote *The War and the International,* a book opposing the war. By November 1914, he had moved to Paris to assume the role of editor for the internationalist socialist newspaper *Nashe Slovo* ("Our Word"). By the end of March 1915, Trotsky was deported from France due to his fervent anti-war stance at his newspaper. He would quickly out-stay his welcome in Spain, and by Christmas day in 1916, Spanish authorities were ready to send Trotsky on his way to New York to simply be rid of him.

But it was not that simple. Originally, Trotsky was to be sent to Havana, Cuba from Spain. Trotsky wanted to go back to Switzerland but was unable due to a lack of funds. He was first incarcerated in Barcelona, yet an unnamed person had arranged for his release and arranged for his subsequent relocation to Cadiz, where Trotsky would await his fate. He spent most of October to December in Cadiz supposedly penniless, complaining to whomever would listen, including Alexander Parvus. This Russo-Germanic socialist, aka the "Merchant of Revolution," had secretly been funding Trotsky via Ernst Bark, another wayward Russian revolutionary. Parvus was steering Trotsky to America for much different reasons.

Alexander Parvus, 1905 (Wikimedia Commons)

Parvus and Trotsky's friendship began in 1904. What drew them together was the theory of "permanent revolution." Trotsky's idea of a "permanent revolution" is explained by how socialist revolutions could occur in societies that had not achieved advanced capitalism. What tore the friends apart (although not completely) in 1915 was Trotsky's belief that his friend was favouring Germany a little too much. While Parvus was indeed a German intelligence asset, he was simultaneously a British one. This stemmed from his arms dealing days in Turkey during the Balkan Wars of 1912 to 1913, when he did business with the British military arms manufacturer Vickers Limited. A pragmatist, Parvus felt that any behaviour or activity which furthered the cause of international socialism was okay as long as the ends were met successfully. The Germans gave Parvus millions of marks to disrupt the Russian war effort by any means available, just as the Germans would later facilitate Lenin's return to Russia.

Trotsky wanted to go to neutral Switzerland, and Parvus wanted Trotsky to be in New York. Parvus had to convince Trotsky that going to the United States was in the best interest of the coming revolution. Parvus's view was more aligned to his German masters because they were willing to do more for him monetarily than his British masters would in furthering his socialist views. America, according to Parvus, with its "enormous number of Jews and Slavs," gave the cause a "very receptive element for anti-Tsarist agitation." And who best to carry out that mission than Leon Trotsky, whose intellect and oratory skills were unmatched at the time? Trotsky's role in America, as defined by Parvus, was to fundraise and spread the word amongst the American proletariat about the coming revolution.

NEW YORK, 1917

The *S.S. Montserrat* docked late on the evening of 13 January 1917 in New York Harbor. When the ship docked, Trotsky seemed happy to be in the "New World," despite the cold, wet, and windy weather. Despite his repeated declarations of poverty, Trotsky landed in New York with several hundred dollars in his possession, which was no small sum at the time. His first-class passage was paid for by Parvus, via Bark, and his first few days were spent at the expensive Hotel Astor, which was close to Times Square.

Trotsky's only known contacts in New York prior to his arrival were the employees at *Novy Mir*, a magazine published by Russian socialist emigres, for which Trotsky had been a contributor. Ludwig Lore, the German-born Jewish editor of the *New Yorker Volkszeitung*, who would become a close friend of Trotsky's, said, "When Trotsky landed here, his name was known only to his countrymen and a handful of German Socialists." So, how did Trotsky end up at one of the most expensive hotels in New

York? Did Alexander Parvus pay for this, or was Trotsky's care in America assigned to others?

News of Trotsky's arrival in socialist circles in New York had been building since early December 1916, when he personally telegraphed his impending arrival to *Novy Mir*, who published the news. According to the Czar's secret police, the Okhrana, (who were active in the United States), as well as Russian, Jewish, and German socialists, anticipated his arrival with much fervor. They held a "grand reception" in his honour, which drew socialists from many other American cities. When the Trotskys left the *S.S. Monsterrat*, they were met by a reporter from *The New York Times.* Described as a socialist and "pacifist editor" who was expelled from several countries, Trotsky was also met by Arthur Concors of the Hebrew Sheltering and Immigrant Aid Society.

The Hebrew Sheltering and Immigrant Aid Society was a charitable organization created to help Jews who arrived in America with little or no means to sustain themselves. Yet, Arthur Concors was not a normal immigrant greeter. He was the "superintendent" of the Society and a member of the board of directors. So, how was it that a man of Concors's stature ended up greeting a Russian socialist at three a.m. on a cold, rainy morning at the New York docks? It seems most likely that Jacob Schiff, head of the investment banking firm of Kuhn, Loeb and Company and also a senior member of the board of directors of the Hebrew Sheltering and Immigrant Aid Society, arranged to have Concors assist Trotsky upon his arrival.

Exactly whom Schiff was assisting is another issue. There was the matter of the oft mentioned ten thousand dollars of German money Trotsky was stated to have left New York with when he returned to Russia after the revolution began. Theories abound that this money came from Schiff. A fervent anti-Czarist, Jacob Schiff was a wealthy banker who funded anyone who could help depose Czar Nicholas II, whose anti-Jewish pogroms against Russian Jews were infamous in their brutality. Schiff, who was of Jewish heritage, even went so far as to loan the Empire of Japan two hundred million dollars through his firm, in order to finance the Japanese war effort in the Russo-Japanese war of 1905 against the hated Czar's Russia. But in 1917, did Schiff give his own money to Trotsky, or did he give Trotsky British government money to aid in removing the Czar from power and keep Russia in the war? If there even was money, which many now doubt, was it given by Schiff at the behest of MI6, or was it actually Schiff's money?

Jacob Schiff (Wikimedia Commons)

Despite these alleged ties and the fact that Schiff was a fervent anti-Czarist activist, he was also a German. Although he had made his considerable fortune in America, he still had significant ties to his homeland. His brothers, Phillip and Ludwig Schiff, were bankers in Germany with connections to the Kaiser. Also, Jacob Schiff's good friend was Max Warburg, Director of M.M. Warburg and Company, a private, family-owned bank. Warburg was also a close friend and adviser to Kaiser Wilhelm II. Warburg had three brothers who were actively pro-German; one worked for the German government, and the other two worked for Schiff in New York.

Schiff and the Warburgs were well known to American and British intelligence. Sir William Wiseman, of Britain's Secret Intelligence Service (later MI6), was on good terms with Schiff and was rumored to have had an informant on the board of Kuhn, Loeb and Co., unbeknownst to his friend. (Wiseman would, not insignificantly, later become a partner in Schiff's firm after the war.)

While it was most unlikely that Schiff and Trotsky had ever met, it was almost certain that Schiff would have sent someone in his place. Was it Arthur Concors, Schiff's fellow board member from the Hebrew Sheltering and Immigrant Aid Society, who acted as the go-between? Or was it Otto Schwarzschild, another recent resident of the Astor who was known to American intelligence as a German spy and who, as an employee of the Schiff-funded Committee for the East, aided Jews in Poland? Possibly it was the Russian-born Salomon Rosenblum, A.K.A. "Ace of Spies" Sidney Reilly, who had been conducting business with Schiff since at least the Russo-Japanese War. Reilly, by contacting Trotsky, would be serving his British master, Sir William Wiseman, as well.

Reilly's New York office was situated at 120 Broadway, in the Equitable Building.

Cropped 1918 passport photo of famous espionage agent Sidney Reilly. This passport was issued under his alias of George Bergmann. (Wikimedia Commons)

This building also housed the Russo-Asiatic Bank (RAB), whose American agent represented the Chinese Eastern Railway (a subsidiary of RAB). Reilly also came into contact with Samuel MacRoberts, who was vice president of the National City Bank and a trustee of the Russian Insurance Company. MacRoberts invited Reilly to be the managing officer of the Allied Machine Company, which was a National City Bank-owned export company. Reilly used his high-ranking position with the Allied Machine Company to shield his duplicitous dealings with his British, American, and German "clients."

One other person had an office at 120 Broadway: Jacob Schiff. This made meetings and possibly money exchanges between the two easier.

Shortly afterwards, Trotsky and his family found a two-bedroom apartment in the Bronx for the princely sum of eighteen dollars per month. Trotsky stated in his autobiography that their new apartment:

> "…was equipped with all sorts of conveniences that we Europeans were quite unused to: electric lights, gas cooking-range, bath, telephone, automatic service-elevator, and even a chute for the garbage. These things completely won the boys over to New York. For a time the telephone was their main interest; we had not had this mysterious instrument in either Vienna or Paris."

Trotsky's wife Natalya paid their rent three months in advance and furnished the apartment "on the installment plan."

Trotsky stated that his "only profession in New York was that of a revolutionary socialist…I wrote articles, edited a newspaper, and addressed labor meetings." Despite pleading poverty throughout much of the previous year, Trotsky move across several countries in Europe, all the while living not an uncomfortable life. After his expulsion from Spain, despite his own admission of being penniless, he and his family travelled first-class to New York aboard the *S.S. Montserrat*. During his two and a half-month stay in New York, estimates of his earnings have ranged from between five hundred and one thousand dollars from his writing for *Novy Mir* and from his lectures. Yet how could he afford an apartment with many modern luxuries in New York City? How was it that Trotsky's wife and children, political refugees from Europe, were chauffeured around the city by the good graces of a certain "Dr. M," whom Trotsky never identified?

Dr. M has since been identified by Bronx historian Lloyd Ultan as Dr. Julius Hammer. Hammer was a Russian Jew, born in

Odessa, who emigrated to the United States in 1875. In time, Dr. Hammer owned, along with his medical practice, the Allied Drug and Chemical Company, which made him a millionaire. He was a member of the American Socialist Labor Party, which was headed by militant Marxist Daniel De Leon. Julius Hammer met Vladimir Lenin at the Seventh Congress of the Second International in 1907, and this meeting served to create a working relationship that lasted until Lenin's death.

"Comrade Hammer," the "American millionaire," was exactly the type of rich Russian-American that Lenin had secretly dispatched Alexandra Kollontai to New York to collect money from, to use "for Russian revolutionary purposes." Kollontai would later be appointed People's Commissar for Social Welfare after the October 1917 Revolution, and in 1923, she was appointed Ambassador to Norway. Hammer did, in fact, give money to Kollontai, and it would be reasonable to assume that Hammer also gave funds to Trotsky. But whether this was the infamous ten thousand dollars is another matter altogether. It seems that Trotsky, Lenin, Alexander Parvus, and others sought as much money from as many sources as possible, and they did not limit themselves to a meagre ten thousand dollars.

Dr. Hammer lived opulently. He lived in a large mansion with servants and a chauffeur, went on grand vacations, and put two sons through university. Most of the money from his business, the Allied Drug and Chemical Company, was used to maintain his lifestyle and fund his political undertakings. It was only through creative accounting and chicanery that Julius Hammer managed to keep his company from going bankrupt. In 1920, Dr. Julius Hammer was sentenced to three and a half years for manslaughter in Sing-Sing for performing an abortion, after which the mother died from complications six days later. There is some speculation that Hammer's son Armand, who was then studying to be a doctor, had actually performed the abortion and that his father was covering up for him. Julius subsequently sent Armand to Russia in his place in 1921 to look after the affairs of his company, the Allied Drug and Chemical Company. Hammer traveled back and forth from the Soviet Union for the next 10 years. Due to his more than ample capabilities, the younger Hammer was "seen as an acceptable front man for Soviet economic enterprises abroad." Armand Hammer embarked upon a lifelong journey caught between communism and the capitalist system that made him rich. All the while, from the beginning, J. Edgar Hoover and the Federal Bureau of Investigation were always lurking in the shadows, watching the younger Hammer's every move.

During his time in New York, Trotsky publicly lectured and wrote. He also attempted to organize an anti-war party from the ranks of the American Socialists, including interested individuals from the German and Russian Federations. Ludwig Lore, in a short missive written in 1918, said, "Trotsky was convinced…that the United States was ripe for the overthrow of the capitalist system." He also stated that Trotsky "urged the calling of general strikes against war as a means of undermining the proud structure of our decaying civilization." Lore further stated that:

> "…Trotsky is born to lead men. His unusual talent as a speaker won the hearts and minds of hearers everywhere. Without pose, strikingly free from the arts and artifices that most speakers use to enhance the effectiveness of their speeches, he was yet able to stir an audience of thousands with the same personal magnetism that made itself so unmistakably felt in the smallest gathering."

Trotsky's oratorical skills, as well as his ability to convey his ideas brilliantly, became as renowned in New York as it had throughout Europe. Russian-born anarchist Emma Goldman, after attending a meeting where Trotsky gave a speech, said:

> "After several rather dull speakers Trotsky was introduced. A man of medium height, with haggard cheeks, reddish hair, and straggling red beard stepped briskly forward. His speech, first in Russian and then in German, was powerful and electrifying. I did not agree with his political attitude; he was a Menshevik (Social Democrat), and as such far removed from us. But his analysis of the causes of the war was brilliant, his denunciation of the ineffective Provisional Government in Russia scathing, and his presentation of the conditions that led up to the Revolution illuminating. He closed his two hours' talk with an eloquent tribute to the working masses of his native land. The audience was roused to a high pitch of enthusiasm, and Sasha and I heartily joined in the ovation given the speaker. We fully shared his profound faith in the future of Russia."

Also at this time, Trotsky became affiliated with and wrote for the Yiddish-language socialist daily newspaper entitled *Forverts* ("Forward"). With a circulation of two hundred thousand copies per day, the newspaper was influential amongst the Jewish emigrants from the Russian Empire. Yet even there, he found himself defending against accusations of being pro-German. Despite being called a German agent, he continued to call for an international socialist revolution amongst the Jewish community he had sought all his life to distance himself from.

When the Zimmerman telegram became public knowledge in the United States in mid-February 1917, *Forverts* and its editor, Abraham Cahan, adopted a pro-American stance. Like the rest of the nation, Cahan was flabbergasted when it became known that the German government was plotting to create a military alliance with Mexico. Mexico, in return and upon the defeat of the Allies, would receive New Mexico, as well as a large portion of California. Trotsky's problem was that Cahan was picking a side in what he called an "imperialist war." Nationalism was a non-starter for Trotsky. Internationalism was all that mattered to him and anything less was unacceptable. Trotsky never wrote for *Forverts* again.

All through January and February, 1917, Trotsky and his "right-hand man" at *Novy Mir* (and subsequent internee in Amherst), Grigori Chudnovski, spoke at meetings throughout New York. Chudnovski was also with Trotsky in Paris and was associated with Alexander Parvus.

Inspector Thomas J. Tunney was the chief inspector with the NYPD's Bomb Squad, a covert task force of about forty detectives whose mission it was to keep eyes on German spies, anarchists, and revolutionaries of all stripes. Tunney quoted Trotsky at one meeting as telling those assembled, "You anarchists here…don't want any militarism or any government which is of no help to the working class, and is always ready to fire on the workman. It's time you did away with such a government once and forever!" Tunney then related that Chudnovski began his speech by stating:

> "Comrades, some of you can't read English. You don't know what is going on until you see it in the Russian papers. Only today I noticed that the police commissioner is going to call out all the reserves he can get to handle the situation, since Germany notified America what she would do. The capitalistic government is *afraid of us!* They are afraid of the working class. Remember that, for in the case of war, we can protest against militarism and start our own war.…"

Thomas J. Tunney, Chief Inspector with the NYPD's Bomb Squad, World War I (extracted from *Throttled! The Detection of the German and Anarchist Bomb Plotters,* Thomas Tunney, Boston: Small, Maynard and Company, 1919)

On 4 March 1917, *The New York Times* described how Trotsky had put forth a motion (which was seconded by Louis Fraina, who became a founding member of the American Communist Party) in which he asked all his comrades present to incite strikes. Should war erupt, everyone was to resist the draft.

44 WHITEHALL AVENUE, NEW YORK

Inspector Tunney and his Bomb Squad were not the only ones interested in Leon Trotsky and his fellow revolutionaries. Prior to the United States' entry into World War I in April 1917, intelligence services from many of the warring countries operated in New York City. Often masked within a country's embassy, the foreign intelligence services of Germany, France, Great Britain, and Russia operated at will with little or no interference from the fledgling American intelligence community.

Great Britain's Secret Intelligence Service (SIS), which was created in 1909, would, under the direction of Commander Mansfield Smith-Cumming, successfully maintain eyes on many players. However, during the war, the SIS focused mainly on the German government's activities. Because Trotsky was an anti-war citizen of an Allied country who had been working toward overthrowing the Russian Government, he came under heavy scrutiny by Britain's MI1(c) (later MI6).

In October 1915, Cummings sent Sir William Wiseman to establish an intelligence bureau called Section V. This Section ensured that German agents could not obstruct the pecuniary and economic support which a neutral America afforded the Allies. There was also the continued agitation of Irish and Indian separatists towards their British masters who had made America their home. The Germans attempted to exploit this situation by extending a helping hand to both groups as a means of stretching British resources.

Yet the most important item on the agenda for Britain was how to get the United States to enter the war. Every means possible was employed to create an atmosphere where the American public, their politicians, and their president's opinion would be in favor of entering the war against Germany. One example of this is the exploitation of the Zimmerman Telegram Affair.

Captain Guy Gaunt was the British Naval Attaché at the British Consulate in New York since January 1914. While he was attached to the Embassy in Washington, D.C., he set up operations within the Consulate offices at 44 Whitehall Street in New York City. With the blessing of Naval Intelligence Division (NID) chief Admiral Reginald "Blinker" Hall, Gaunt began to assemble a network of agents to protect British interests in America.

Gaunt was not of any disposition to allow anyone to take over his role as chief spy in New York. Yet Cummings, whose word carried the most weight with regards to British intelligence, insisted that Wiseman would be in charge. So, who was William Wiseman?

Sir William Wiseman (Wikimedia Commons)

Sir William Wiseman, 10th Baronet, was born in Great Britain in 1885. Sir William decided not to follow in the family tradition of naval service. Instead, he attended Cambridge as a bantam-weight boxer, a playwright, and a journalist before finally settling upon a career in finance.

When war broke out in 1914, Sir William was Chairman of Hendens Trust in London, vice president of two Canadian firms, and director of two more in Great Britain. Early in the war, Sir William's vision became compromised, and he was found unfit for duty. It is not known why Sir William was chosen for his assignment in New York, but it is known that he received "special training" from Scotland Yard.

Wiseman chose as his second in command Captain Norman Thwaites. He was familiar with the United States, could speak German, and was familiar with German society in America. While at university in Germany, Thwaites specialized in journalism. After graduation, he went to America, and by 1905, he was personal assistant to newspaperman Joseph Pulitzer. Thwaites was also Wiseman's connection to NYPD Bomb Squad leader Thomas Tunney, as well as to high ranking officials in the United States Army's Military Intelligence Division.

Wiseman and Thwaites employed a vast number of agents and assets to achieve their various intelligence objectives. People from within and outside of the British government were enlisted for propaganda and publicity work; there was someone to handle code work, and to control the less than reputable detective agencies that were often employed for the more unseemly work.

A man attached to the Anglo-Russian Sub-Committee, created to administer Russian munitions contracts, was paid for with British loans. This same man counselled many of the Czar's officials within the committee, with whom he had been acquainted, whenever difficulties arose. The Russian Supply Committee (RSC), which was responsible for purchasing munitions and war materials for Russia, was also a cause for the utmost concern. Because of corruption within the RSC, it became an easy target for enemy agents and influence peddlers like Sidney Reilly.

Wiseman and Thwaites often segregated their networks, whereas double agents were often utilized to penetrate the good graces of a particular German agent. Much of what Wiseman and his deputy attempted was done without anyone else's knowledge; even services like MI5 were often left out of the loop.

Although he was actually a grifter and confidence man as well as a spy, Reilly was connected to Trotsky and Wiseman in many ways. About Reilly, Thwaites stated that, "his appearance was remarkable.... Complexion swarthy, a long straight nose, piercing eyes, black hair brushed back from a forehead suggesting keen intelligence." He felt that Reilly was "a man that impressed one with a good deal of power." A master of at least seven languages who could change identities on demand, "not only had he charming manners, but he was a most agreeable companion with a fund of information in many spheres."

Reilly was unscrupulous, greedy, disloyal, and he bartered information as well as influence. He became a millionaire, drug smuggler, gun runner, forger, blackmailer, bigamist, and murderer. Reilly biographer, Richard Spence wrote that he was "not all that he claimed, (and) he was often more than he seemed."

Reilly, whom Ian Fleming is said to have modelled Agent 007 after, once stated that "James Bond is just a piece of nonsense I dreamed up. He's not a Sidney Reilly, you know." A virulent anti-Bolshevik, Reilly felt that he could topple Lenin and Trotsky and replace them with himself. Thwaites later observed, "Behind all Reilly's efforts lay the conviction that someday he was destined to bring Russia out of the slough and chaos of Communism. He believed that he would do for Russia what Napoleon had done for France." This was Sidney Reilly—the man with the Napoleon complex.

In 1915, Reilly, through his directorship of Allied Machinery of New York, was engaged in a contract to supply arms and munitions for the Russian Government. Allied Machinery received that contract from Abram Zhivotovski, a Russian with deep connections to many banks and governments. At the time, Zhivotovski was being investigated by the Russians for possible links to the German government. Reilly had already been pegged as a German agent by the Russians. It was suspected but not yet proven that, as the arms and munitions made their way from America to Russia, a stop-off was pre-arranged in Sweden, where a portion of the cargo was diverted, for a handsome profit, to Germany.

Zhivotovski was a Bolshevik sympathizer who had laundered large sums of money on their behalf through his office in Japan. His office was operated by his nephew, who at one point was Reilly's personal secretary. He was also, in fact, Trotsky's cousin. The elder Zhivotovski was Trotsky's uncle—his mother's brother.

Reilly also had strong ties to Alexander Weinstein (who worked for Zhivotovski in London) and Antony Jechalski, who was said to be "a most dangerous German spy" with strong connections to officials of the Russian Supply Committee. Late in the fall of 1916, both Reilly, who was in Japan, and Jechalski, who was in Havana, rushed back to New York about the time Trotsky arrived.

Sidney Reilly seemed to have his hand everywhere. He arranged munitions deals and was paid a commission for his services. According to the SIS, up until 1917, Reilly had made nearly two million dollars. He was also owed an equal amount that would never be repaid, so he would often extract his "pound of flesh" in other ways when he had to. In one case, he arranged a deal to have Remington rifles sold to the Russians. Remington subsequently reneged on paying Reilly his commission since their financial situation was dire. Uncharacteristically and to the utter surprise to all parties involved, instead of suing Remington, Reilly forgave the owing amount in favor of future business.

In another case, the Canadian Car and Foundry Company secured a large munitions contract with the Russian Government with Reilly's help. Due to financial difficulties, the CC&F Company was drastically behind on the delivery of their contract and were experiencing difficulty obtaining more funding from banker J.P. Morgan. Because of this, Reilly was informed that he would not be receiving his commission.

On 11 January 1917, CC&F Company's munition plant in Kingsland, New Jersey was destroyed in a fire. The subsequent explosions totally destroyed the plant without even one death. The company lost three hundred thousand shrapnel rounds, plus the pieces for one million more, as well as two million pounds of TNT. The CC&F Company's insurance paid out enough to save the company and ensure that Reilly received his long-awaited commission.

Officially, blame for the destruction of the plant fell to a German saboteur. However, the plans to destroy the plant were known to some, including Wiseman and Thwaites and a man who worked for them, Casimir Pilenas Palmer. Despite Palmer's warnings to Thwaites, the plant was destroyed, as it seems it was supposed to.

RUSSIAN REVOLUTION

On 15 March 1917, Czar Nicholas II abdicated the Russian throne. The Russian revolution had begun. The news was immediately known by Trotsky as well as the rest of New York City. Trotsky and *Novy Mir* were inundated with media requests. Trotsky would reminisce in his autobiography that, "For a time our paper was the centre of interest of the New York press."

News then arrived from Russia that a provisional government headed by a liberal aristocrat, Prince Georgy Yevgenyevich Lvov, had come into power. He was aided by Alexander Kerensky as Minister of War and by new Foreign Minister Pavel Miliukov, an old nemesis of Trotsky's. Miliukov was Bolshevism's political opponent and he attempted to discredit and destroy it as well as by attempting to have Trotsky smeared with the stain of German money during World War I. In an interview with *The New York Times*, published on 16 March 1917, Trotsky said:

> "...the committee which has taken the place of the deposed Ministry in Russia did not represent the interests or the aims of the revolutionists, that it would probably be short lived and step down in favor of men who would be more sure to carry forward the democratization of Russia."

Those men Trotsky spoke of were the Mensheviks and the Bolsheviks. Now he needed to be able to return from exile abroad and return home to Russia. Trotsky set about doing so.

Due to the fractious nature of Russian politics at this time, Russia had a "dual power" structure after the abdication of the Czar. On one side was the provisional government made up of an army general, a prince, and the leader of the Constitutional Democratic Party, called the Kadets. The Kadets were fully committed to full citizenship for all of Russia's minorities and supported Jewish emancipation. Another much larger group, the Provisional Soviet Council of Workers and Soldiers Deputies—which included Mensheviks, Soviet revolutionaries, and a few Bolsheviks—did not believe that the nation was yet ready for socialism. They were prepared to work for the introduction of a republic, basic civil and human rights, a legitimate and non-corrupt police and army, and the elimination of ethnic and religious persecution.

The "dual power" made governing nearly impossible. While the provisional government sought to please as many of the Soviets as it could, inevitably, the political situation became increasingly more fractious. This situation spilled over to New York. Immediately, most of the Russian diplomatic corps in the embassies and consuls throughout the United States recognized the new provisional government.

However, another group attempted to usurp the powers of the Russian Supply Committee (RSC); they claimed they wished to take control over "all Russian assets and agencies on American soil," should it please the new provisional government. They were seen as "an unofficial and self-appointed body" which justified its existence, at least publicly, by saying they were an advisory board awaiting instructions from Petrograd.

Dr. Nikolai G. Kuznetsov, a onetime member of the RSC and spokesman for the new group, who spoke those words to *The New York Times* on 17 March 1917, promptly recanted them in the same paper the next day. He said "a certain Russian with large business and official connections in Russia" had called him up earlier in the day and, incensed by the report of what the committee proposed to do, threatened to "knock my head off" if he became involved with such an enterprise. Kuznetsov said that the man also threatened to make trouble for him with the Russian Government.

This unnamed man, who most certainly sounds like Sidney Reilly, was "said to be engaged in an enterprise to put American automobiles on the Russian market and command an illegitimately high price for them by pretending they were manufactured in Russia, where the cost of material was higher than in the United States." This seems plausible as Henry Ford was smart enough to know that he could ship "knocked down" cars cheaper than sending them whole or building from scratch in foreign countries. As for excessive profits, this may have had as much to do with Reilly as it did Ford; everyone wanted to make as much profit as the market could handle.

Kuznetsov was an automobile specialist and instructor at the Petrograd Military Institute; his other specialty was tractors. Why would he sabotage that deal in the press for Sidney Reilly? Maybe his dealings with the Russian Supply Committee were enough to sever any commission he may have had a chance to enjoy from the deal. In the same article, Kuznetsov also said that he was not afraid of this man because of his own knowledge of this deal.

Who was the automobile manufacturer referred to in *The New York Times* by Kuznetsov? Henry Ford had been aggressively expanding his manufacturing empire for some time. Ford had previously targeted Russia for expansion, especially for his tractors, which represented a massive opportunity because of the agrarian nature of Russia. Ford believed that international trade was essential to world peace. After his ill-fated "Peace Ship" mission in 1915, the attempt to foster anti-war sentiment throughout Europe that cost him five hundred thousand dollars, Ford said, "I didn't get much peace, but I heard in Norway that Russia might well become a huge market for tractors soon."

The deal with Reilly had been in the works for some time, and with the arrival of the Russian revolution, the situation became more precarious for the completion and execution of the deal. Henry Ford was worried about threats, real or perceived, to his business interests and would take any measures to protect them. Whether that meant invoking his friendship with Woodrow Wilson or dealing with one of the main players in the Russian revolution, who happened to be Jewish, meant little to the antisemitic Ford, who had so much at stake.

Ford was notorious for using detective agencies whenever the need arose. Ernest Liebold, Ford's personal secretary, created an extensive secret network of ex–United States Secret Service and Army Intelligence officers to fulfill their needs. At the height of their antisemitic dealings, a German detective they hired to communicate with the ex-Kaiser after the war warned Liebold to be careful with any communications. He said, "I have no delusions about what the Jewish revolutionary party in Germany will do to me if they find out that I am communicating with the Hohenzollerns on behalf of Mr. Ford, in order to secure information that will show the Jews up." Although it occurred after the war, this incident exemplified the measures Ford was willing to take to achieve his ends. He was faced with having to negotiate with the Jewish Bronstein, aka Leon Trotsky, who would be sequestered in a prisoner of war camp in Amherst, Nova Scotia, Canada.

With the coming of the revolution, the landscape was changing rapidly. For Trotsky, the announcement that all exiles could return home must have felt like manna from Heaven for the committed socialist internationalist. For Wiseman and the British, the potential for Russia's removal from the war due to the anti-war sensibilities of the Bolsheviks caused much strategic re-thinking. Both had much work to do and little time to accomplish their tasks.

The Russian American diaspora of New York City in March 1917 was awash with more spies, double agents, Czarists, anti-Czarists, profiteers, collaborators, radical editors, writers, and socialists than one could ever imagine. In the midst of this there were German, Turkish, British, American, French, and Russian national interests colliding during a war which had been consuming the Western world. Then the Russian revolution, which began on 15 March 1917, sent exiled Russians scurrying back home, Trotsky included.

Trotsky, according to his autobiography, visited the Russian Consul-General's office in New York. He said:

> "By that time the portrait of Czar Nicholas had been removed from the wall, but the heavy atmosphere of a Russian police station under the old regime still hung about the place. After the usual delays and argument, the Consul-General ordered that papers be issued to me for the passage to Russia. In the British consulate, as well, they told me, when I filled out the questionnaire, that the British authorities would put no obstacles in the way of my return to Russia. Everything was in good order."

Little did he know what lay ahead.

With the Russian Revolution now in progress, the landscape ahead looked much different for both Germany and the Allied powers. The prospect of no Russian front meant different things to the belligerents. To Germany, it meant they would be able to theoretically divert a million of their troops from the Eastern front to the Western front, quite possibly ending the war within months. All it cost them was a few million marks and safe passage aboard a sealed train for Vladimir Lenin from Switzerland to Petrograd.

For the British and the rest of the Allies, the potential exit of the Russian army meant possible defeat. Lenin wanted to take Russia out of the war; Trotsky did not. Publicly, Trotsky did not want a separate peace, and he wanted to continue fighting the Germans if it meant protecting the revolution. In the pages of *Novy Mir*, Trotsky wrote a piece that must have pleased Wiseman and his British masters plenty. Trotsky wrote:

> "The Russian revolution (so he answered the critics) represents an infinitely greater danger to the Hohenzollern than do the appetites and designs of imperialist Russia. The sooner the revolution throws off the chauvinist mask, which the Grickhovs and Milinkovs have forced upon her, and the sooner we reveal her true proletariat face, the more powerful will be the response she meets in Germany and the less will be the Hohenzollern's desire and capacity to strangle the Russian revolution, the more will he have of his own domestic trouble.

> "But what will happen (the critic asks) if the German proletariat fails to rise? What are you going to do then?

"You suppose, then, that the Russian revolution can take place without affecting Germany? But this is altogether improbable.

"Still, what if this were nevertheless to be the case?

"Really, we need not rack our brains over so implausible a supposition. The war has transformed the whole of Europe into a powder magazine of social revolution. The Russian proletariat is now throwing a flaming torch into that powder magazine. To suppose that this will cause no explosion is to think against the laws of historical logic and psychology. Yet if the improbable were to happen, if the conservative, social-patriotic organization were to prevent the German working class from rising against its ruling classes in the near future, then, of course, the Russian working class would defend the revolution arms in hand…and wage war against the Hohenzollern, and call upon the fraternal German proletariat to rise against the common enemy…. The task would be to defend not the fatherland but the revolution and to carry it to other countries."

This was the type of man the British could have used to their benefit.

Sir William Wiseman went to great lengths to gather information on Trotsky. Wiseman needed, with the arrival of the Russian revolution, to create a unique intelligence and propaganda service in Russia. Great Britain's interests needed to be served and Germany's needed to be thwarted. He needed to "guide the storm" in Russia, and he needed as many resources there to ensure that the Russian army stayed in the field.

Wiseman managed to secure seventy-five thousand dollars from the American government with the help of President Woodrow Wilson's closest advisor, Colonel Edward House. With that money in hand, Wiseman was able to secure an additional seventy-five thousand dollars from Jacob Schiff. Britain and the Allies were not looked upon favourably in Russia during this period, so money that came from a man like Schiff fit Wiseman's purposes perfectly. With this money, Wiseman sent many pro-Allied exiles to Russia as counter-measures to the German pacifist propaganda efforts to guide Russia out of the war.

Wiseman, following the lead of the British War Cabinet, also allied himself with as many Zionists as possible. The Zionists, who had longed for a national home in Palestine, were being encouraged to keep Russia in the war in exchange for their long-desired goal. Of all the members of the British War Cabinet, William Churchill was the most vocal in his support of the Jewish homeland. In March 1915, an Anglo-French task force attempted a naval bombardment of Turkish defences in the Dardanelles. In April, the Mediterranean Expeditionary Force, including the Australian and New Zealand Army Corp (ANZAC), began its assault at Gallipoli. Both of these campaigns failed and Churchill was held by many MPs, particularly Conservatives, to be personally responsible. He would lose his position as First Lord of the Admiralty in 1915 due to his debacle in the Gallipoli campaign. By 1917 he was back in the cabinet as Minister of Munitions.

William Wiseman, while part of MI1c in New York, was publicly assigned to the Transport Department of the Ministry of Munitions. This was the same Ministry Churchill headed. He may have had a hand in having Trotsky released, or at least was instrumental in aiding the British in exchange for free passage to Russia while he was imprisoned in Amherst.

To aid him in obtaining support in Russia, Wiseman turned to his friend Sidney Reilly, who was a Russian Jew. While Reilly worked that end, Wiseman was busy exploiting the American-based Jews for as much support and money as possible. He turned to Jacob Schiff, the German American Jewish banker, who was free with his money when it came to helping the Jews of Russia. Schiff also had important connections with Russian bankers, who could help mask the fact that much of the money was coming to them from the Allied nations. The Allies were not looked upon favourably in Russia due to their poor treatment of the Russian army and the deprivations that the populace had to endure during the war.

Wiseman, who had no experience with or knowledge of Russia, turned to a man who had none either—but at least he spoke Russian and had rudimentary experience as a spy. Somerset Maugham, the writer, who was related to Wiseman through marriage, said Wiseman told him that the "long and short of it was that I should go to Russia and keep the Russians in the war." He ultimately had no effect on the outcome in Russia, nor would Schiff and his millions. The only hope Wiseman had was that of all the agents he had, "a well-known international socialist" agent that he had in place held the most promise—or so he thought.

Meanwhile, Trotsky, "a well-known international socialist," was waiting for the proper paperwork to arrive in order to leave America and he grew more agitated daily. Word from Russia indicated that the Mensheviks (at this point, Trotsky still was one) and the Socialist-Revolutionaries seemed amenable to supporting the Provisional Government, which wanted to continue the war the same way Czar Nicholas had. About the Provisional Government, Trotsky said:

> "By the grace of the Revolution which they had not wanted and which they had fought, Guchkov [Minister of War] and Milukov [Minister of Foreign Affairs] are now in power. For the continuation of the war, for victory? Of course! They are the same persons who had dragged the country into the war for the sake of the interests of capitol. All their opposition to Czarism had its source in their unsatisfied imperialistic appetites. So long as the clique of Nicholas II was in power, the interests of the dynasty and of the reactionary nobility were prevailing in Russian foreign affairs. This is why Berlin and Vienna had hoped to conclude a separate peace with Russia. Now purely imperialistic interests have superseded the Czarism interests; pure imperialism is written on the banner of the Provisional Government. "The government of the Czar is gone," the Milukovs and the Guchkovs say to the people. "Now you must shed your blood for the common interests of the entire nation."

Trotsky wanted no part of an alliance with the provisional government. He wanted no part of a separate peace with Germany. (This was music to Wiseman's ears as it was the Allies goal to keep the Russians in the war, thus maintaining a two-front war..) A separate peace would do great harm to his "international socialist" view of the world. Trotsky needed the German proletariat to rise up at the same time and throw off the imperialistic Hohenzollerns. A separate peace would not be pleasing for the cause.

While in America, Trotsky did his best to campaign against those who had hoped that the Americans would join the war. One more nation added to the world war was not what Trotsky wanted or needed. Inspector Thomas Tunney of the NYPD Bomb Squad kept a close watch on Trotsky, Chudnovski, and the other revolutionaries around New York City. Tunney related in his autobiography that, on 26 March 1917, a farewell meeting was held for Trotsky at the Harlem River Casino. He said:

> "Some 800 people were at Trotsky's farewell party, which was held under the auspices of the German Socialist Federation. Alexander Berkman and Emma Goldman were among those present. A blond Russian made a speech in which he said: 'Comrades, some of us are going back to Russia to push the revolution as we think it ought to be pushed, and those who remain here must get ready to do their share of the work as it ought to be done.' Trotsky then rose and speaking first in German, then in Russian, repeated the advice the previous speaker had given, and added: 'You who stay here must work hand in hand with the revolution in Russia, for only in that way can you accomplish revolution in the United States.' He was cheered to the echo."

Tunney was scathing in his final assessment of Trotsky. He said Trotsky was "an undersized, wild-eyed, fanatic little plucked-bantam of a Russian expatriate literally set out from Hoboken to upset the provisional government of Russia, prevent the formation of a republic, stop the war with Germany, and prevent interference from other governments—that was his open boast. And, if such a mission can be crowned with success, he succeeded."

The aroma of German money kept sticking to Trotsky despite his protestations to the contrary. There were dozens, if not hundreds of different ways that money could have made it to Russia and as many people to accomplish it with, not to mention with Leon Trotsky. Now while he may have thought it reprehensible to take money from the Germans, the British, or the Americans, Trotsky was pragmatic enough to take money from whoever offered it. He was smart enough to find a way to keep it and not to get caught. Well, almost.

Wiseman relied on, when it came to Trotsky, a Russian born, ex-Scotland Yard and Okhrana spy named Casimir Pilenas-Palmer. After becoming too well known while working on the 1910 Houndstitch Murders in London, Pilenas fled England for New York City and assumed the name Palmer. By 1916, he was employed by Wiseman primarily as a spy on German agents. It was a report by Pilenas, given to Wiseman, that subsequently informed his immediate superiors in London on 22 March that Trotsky was in possession of Jewish money "behind which are possibly Germans."

Three days later, on 25 March 1917, Trotsky travelled to the British Consulate at 44 Whitehall Street to pick up his transit visa. The Passport Control Section was under the immediate supervision of Norman Thwaites, who worked directly for Wiseman. Since Trotsky would be sailing to Norway, he needed to pass an inspection at Halifax, Nova Scotia because of the British blockade of Germany. Trotsky wrote, shortly after finally arriving in Petrograd, that Consular officials in New York told him that "British officials would put no obstacles in the way of my return to Russia," and they "assured me that I had complied with all formalities and could make my journey without any difficulties."

In the months after the October revolution, many questions began to surface about Trotsky's time in New York. Considering the prominent role he played in the revolution and the ever-present odor of German money, the attorney general of the United States Department of Justice ordered an investigation. Assigned to examine this issue was Deputy Attorney General Alfred Becker. In a summary of his report, which was made public on 19 January 1918 and reported by *The New York Times* on 20 January, Becker stated that $1394.50 had been spent on steamship tickets for the group of Russian exiles going back to Russia. The tickets were purchased by Trotsky himself. This issue would arise later in Halifax, given as a reason for Trotsky's arrest.

Becker said, with regards to this issue, "the steamship tickets were paid for in currency, and while Trotsky acted as spokesman most of his companions accompanied him to the agency office, and the steamship's recollection is that each one paid for his own ticket, and that Trotsky collected the money from them in the office." Becker also noted that he had spoken to the Russian Consul, who said,

> "…at the time Trotsky left he made application to the Consul for funds, but it seems that the Russian Government had not made provision at that time for the proper credits for Russian emigrants, and that while Trotsky did not get any funds from the Russian Government it seems that a few weeks after Trotsky departed proper credits were arranged for in New York, and up to this date Russians desiring to return to Russia can secure free passage at the Consulate upon application."

It seemed that Trotsky needed funds for the final leg of his journey. Or did he? Was this a ploy to throw investigators or spies off his scent? Was he really poor, or did he ascribe to the notion that he didn't have to use his own money when others would do quite nicely? We may never know if he had German money, British money, American money, or even Jewish money. It seems possible that it was a combination of the above. One thing for sure is that the "revolution" needed money, and a large part of socialist operations in America was fundraising. So it seems probable that Trotsky had raised funds for the cause. It is just as probable that other arrangements were made for the money to move to Russia. Trotsky was pragmatic.

Becker's final word on Trotsky's time in New York are as follows: "I have been unable to verify any indications of Trotsky's receiving money from any German sources."

The scene which played out on the South Brooklyn docks was memorable for Trotsky. On 27 March, with his family and fellow revolutionaries in tow, the group began to board the *S.S. Kristianiafjord* in preparation for the long voyage back to Russia. According to Ludwig Lore, with "rain…falling in torrents, some three hundred well-wishers, carrying red flags and flowers, showed up to bid farewell." Inspector Tunney of the NYPD Bomb Squad characterized it as "a strange sight." Lore continued by stating that "when Trotsky arrived he was lifted to the shoulders of his admirers and with beaming face and happy smile he bade farewell to the comrades…."

Trotsky said, "We had been sent off in a deluge of flowers and speeches. We had passports and visas. Revolution, flowers and visas were balm to our nomad souls."

Also boarding the *S.S. Kristianiafjord* was William G. Shepherd, a journalist who had worked for the United Press during the Great War. His resume included following future Mexican President Francisco Madero throughout his successful revolution in Mexico in 1910. He was present when the United States Marines went ashore during the Battle of (and subsequent occupation of) Vera Cruz, Mexico in 1914. At the beginning of the Great War, Shepherd interviewed Winston Churchill, First Lord of the Admiralty, who had not given an interview in many years. It was a major coup for the veteran journalist.

William G. Shepherd
(https://shootingthegreatwar.blogspot.com/2017/06/)

Shepherd was travelling to Russia to cover the revolution for the publication *Everybody's Magazine*; he had booked passage aboard the *Kristianiafjord*, which was why he was present during the send-off festivities. He wrote that as he drew closer to the pier, many "squares of red-tissue came into view.... These pieces of paper were attached to canes. The canes were waved in the air. The red-tissue paper crackled stiffly." He prophetically continued by proclaiming, "... the dread red flag!" He told his readers that, as he wrote about the one hundred and fifty people gathered at the pier, (many of whom were revolutionaries and anarchists heading to Russia), "New York did not know what we (meaning all of the passengers) had in our heads. And if it had known what some of us had in our hearts and throats and pockets, it would probably have called a policeman and had the law on us."

Shepherd continued, "It created uneasy stirrings in your mind, reminding you of presidential assassinations, Haymarket riots, and all manner of slaughters." And then he said, "No wonder some of our pockets had been hidden to the gaze of New York!" Even then, to someone not in "the know" when it came to the dealings and counter-dealings of spies and double agents, Shepherd was in-tune to the people who gathered at that South Brooklyn pier to travel to Norway.

S.S. Kristianiafjord (Wikimedia Commons)

The *S.S. Kristianiafjord* carried more than Trotsky, his family, and a few revolutionaries, though. The ship's manifest reveals many people who deserve further scrutiny. Among those arrested with Trotsky in Halifax was Gregori Chudnovski, previously described as his right-hand man in New York, Leiba Fisheleff, and Nikita Muchin. Also connected to Trotsky and aboard the *Kristianiafjord* was Robert Zhivotovski, who was his cousin, and Israel J. Fundaminsky, whom Trotsky categorized as a spy for the British.

Another passenger was a former Russian Ambassador to the United States, Andrei Kalpaschnikoff. He grew up in Imperial Russia's upper class, and while fighting in the war, he was promoted to Director of the Russian Red Cross. While attempting to procure ambulances for the Russian Army in New York, he was linked with other pro-Czarist individuals like Sidney Reilly and Russian Vice Consul Peter Rutskii. Kalpaschnikoff also served as a British translator for Trotsky while in Halifax. He paid for that affiliation after the October Revolution; Trotsky, as head of the Red Army, had him arrested and imprisoned for his collaboration with the British in Halifax.

Another person aboard the *S.S. Kristianiafjord* was Charles R. Crane, who had inherited his vast fortune from his bathroom fixture magnate father. Crane was an avid Russophile and Arabist who was, consequently, an anti-Semite. He was a friend of Henry Ford, and in later years, like Ford, he became an admirer of Adolf Hitler.

Crane was well aware who Trotsky was when he boarded the *Kristianiafjord*. He knew that Trotsky was Jewish and that he was part of a cabal that wanted to destroy the Russia he loved. In his unpublished memoirs, written in the early 1930s, Crane said, "Although Trotsky was supposed to be on the other end of the scale from the great bankers of Israel, he nevertheless had had a secret meeting with the chief of them and started off well financed for his venture." Crane was referring to Jacob Schiff. He may have received this information from his son, Richard, who was personal secretary to United States Secretary of State Robert Lansing. Often, information that went to his son also went to his father, with President Woodrow Wilson's blessing.

Charles Crane (Wikimedia Commons)

Charles Crane was also an avid supporter and confidante of President Woodrow Wilson. Shortly after leaving for Russia, Wilson appointed Crane as a member of the Root Commission, which was tasked with trying to arrange American co-operation with the new Russian provisional government. The United States became the first country to formally recognize the new provisional government, and Crane was instrumental in swaying Wilson. In his final correspondence with Wilson before leaving for Russia, Crane commented on how wonderful it was that Wilson was "so well and serene. The example of the White House is an immense steadying power that can be felt all over the country." While thinking of China, Crane mused to Wilson, "I do not know about the men at present in control of the political destinies of China, but I do know that the men in the provisional government of Russia are the best group running any one of the great powers."

Charles Crane had invited journalist Lincoln Steffens to journey with him to Russia. Crane wanted to have Steffens report on the Russian situation in a biased and sympathetic fashion to the American public. Of Crane, Steffens stated:

"He knows everybody. He is 'the friend of Russia' in the United States.... He has entertained all the great Russians, including Milyukov, whom he has had as his guest here and in Chicago. And all the great radicals have had his aid. He (and I with him) will walk into the inner circles of the new government and the new radical party; into the old court group and the new nobility. I will be able to get the whole story up to date and be in on the next phase of it personally!"

Lincoln Steffens (Wikimedia Commons)

Steffens was friends with figures like Teddy Roosevelt, Woodrow Wilson, Ernest Hemingway, Jimmy Cagney, and James Joyce. As publisher of McClure's Magazine, Steffens was one of the original three muckrakers, investigative journalists who were reform-minded and did much to influence American politics. His book *Shame of the Cities* (1904) tackled the corruption of local politics, and his investigation of terrible business practices helped create the Federal Reserve. He covered the 1910 bombing of the Los Angeles Times, and he covered the Mexican Revolution in 1914. He reported on the Versailles Peace Treaty of 1919, and two years later, while on a diplomatic mission to Russia, he interviewed Vladimir Lenin.

While at sea, Steffens engaged Trotsky about Petrograd and Russia. Steffens categorized this on-board discussion as follows: "We all agree that the revolution is in its first phase only," and "we shall be in Petrograd for the re-revolution."

Steffens stayed on friendly terms with Trotsky after this voyage. He penned the foreword to Trotsky's 1918 edition of his book *War and the International,* and for a while, he was a supporter of the Bolsheviks. When speaking of the Russian Revolution in 1919, Steffens famously stated, "I have seen the future and it works."

A Communist journalist was not what Charles Crane had in mind when he brought him along. Crane complained that Steffens and William Shepherd were showing Trotsky and the other Russian revolutionaries a large amount of sympathy.

Meanwhile, as the *S.S. Kristianiafjord* was stilled docked in South Brooklyn, William Shepherd wrote later that: "We who were to sail went aboard; those who were not remained on the pier. The crowd ashore cheered at the crowd aboard." The "song of the International Socialists of Europe" was sung. Shepherd wrote that speeches made quayside sounded like "strange Russian cries," and onboard the *S.S. Kristianiafjord,* he said it was like "an anarchist meeting." Feeling the nervousness of the non-revolutionaries aboard, Shepherd said, "Folks have been arrested for less than this."

As the *S.S. Kristianiafjord* cleared the New York harbor, Shepherd was still wondering about the revolutionaries that remained in New York City. He asked, tongue firmly in cheek:

> "[What about] those red flags back in New York! Those people who carried them secretly in their pockets, and who sang that strange song! You can't forget them. They keep you awake. We know their secrets. Somewhere among the city's million chambers they have distributed themselves with their red flags and their dangerous ideal. Ought not good, loyal Americans to send a wireless back to New York telling it what danger lies hidden in its midst? Ought not the New York police to send out a red-flag manhunt through the streets, alleys, and houses of the city this very night? One must not let this red flag business go too far. All the Russian anarchist and nihilist business that men write thrilling plays about and put into books isn't a pretty sight in the good old United States, and these people here on the boat who have come from Lord-knows-what byways and basements of America, and those people we left behind there on the wharf with their flags and their song, are cheek-to-jowl with all that sort of thing."

Shepherd, once at sea with the rest of the people aboard the *S.S. Kristianiafjord*, began to tell the reader about life amongst the radicals. He related the story of Mrs. Bigni-Schlachta, whom everybody simply called Bigni-Schlachta. She could "play poker like a whole gambling house" and was "the quietest, prettiest girl on the boat." She had travelled the United States as part of a dance troupe and was often seen on the second-class deck, "hovering about a certain deck-chair where was stretched a quiet, thin man [Trotsky] with a straggly, uncertain beard." Shepherd assured the reader, "It was not with coquetry that Bigni-Schlachta hovered but with respect." He reported that she was not the only one who had been hovering. It seemed all the Russians congregated on the second-class deck, and "if the thin-faced man chose to talk, gather around him and listen. But they would merely walk up and down past him if he seemed to prefer a reverie."

Shepherd related that no one in New York City had known who this man was, "but he had things in his past, that man, to hold reverie about." He finally told the reader that the man was Trotsky. "It was he! Speak his name anywhere in Russia in the old days of Czardom or now; in the Czar's palace, in dark offices of bureaucrats, or in the peasant's hut, and it would cause a thrill." Shepherd related the story of what happened in 1905 on Bloody Sunday in Russia. (Bloody Sunday is the name given to the events of Sunday, 22 January 1905 in St. Petersburg, Russia when unarmed demonstrators, led by Father Georgy Gapon were fired upon by soldiers of the Imperial Guard as they marched towards the Winter Palace to present a petition to Czar Nicholas II of Russia. Some view the events of Bloody Sunday to be one of the key events which led to the Russian Revolution of 1917.) Shepherd wrote that if that event had happened in the recent past [the October Revolution was still six months into the future], "this thin, tired-faced man in the deck chair would have been one of the masters of vast and holy Russia. Instead, he has only been hiding somewhere in the United States after escaping from Siberia."

Charles Crane may have been correct. Maybe Shepherd had been influenced by the persuasive and magnetic Russian revolutionary. Shepherd continued his characterization of Trotsky by writing that:

"He [Trotsky] knows men who have made dark and high assassinations; in all those black Russian mysteries, out of which we create books and plays, he has had his part. What he has wanted and suffered for all his life, what his friends have died for, has come to pass. He has dreamed of the New Russia, and the New Russia has come. Astounding planet! A man with a dream like that, come true, does not have many feelings that may be expressed in words.

"So, he lay in the sunshine, speaking little, playing now and then with three little Norwegian children from Philadelphia, who couldn't understand his talk, but who seemed to understand his smile, and waited, with the rest of us, for the boat to reach Halifax."

Lincoln Steffens reflected fourteen years later in his autobiography that the "passenger list was long and mysterious. Trotsky was in the steerage with a group of revolutionaries. There was a Japanese revolutionist in my cabin. There were a lot of Dutch hurrying home from Java, the only innocent people aboard. The rest were war messengers, two from Wall Street to Germany...."

Crane said, "We had a motley lot of passengers, many of them spies of the greatest keenness traveling under assumed names. There was a wonderful battle of wits going on all the time, each one wondering who everyone really was and what his game might be."

On 28 March 1917, while the *S.S. Kristianiafjord* was still en route to Halifax, a telegram was sent from the British consul in New York to Admiral Reginald "Blinker" Hall of the Naval Intelligence Division (NID) and MI5. It said, "An important movement has been started here among Socialists, with a view to getting back Revolutionary Socialists into Russia...with the object of establishing a Republic and initiating peace movement; also of promoting Socialistic Revolutions in other countries, including the United States." It also said that Trotsky was the "main leader" and that "there are Russian Socialists leaving for the purpose of starting revolution against present Russian Government for which Trotsky is reported to have $10,000 subscribed by Socialists and Germans."

British naval attaché Guy Gaunt added, "I am notifying Halifax to hold [Trotsky and associates] until they receive your instructions." It seems probable that Gaunt issued the order at Wiseman's request. Wiseman had the information, yet Gaunt, who held no fondness for Wiseman and would take any opportunity available to discredit his MI6 counterpart, had quicker access to naval authorities in Halifax. With that access, he could keep Trotsky until assurances could be made, or simply to make his story that he was detained by the British a little stronger once back in Russia. All Wiseman had to do was have Pilenas feed the information to Gaunt, and the rest would take care of itself.

The critical role that the Russian army played in the war is the centerpiece to all the conspiratorial dealings of both the Germans and the British. It was important for both the Allies and the Central Powers to have assets in place within the many revolutionary factions in Russia. For Trotsky, the constant subterfuge and conspiratorial escapades were definitely a means to an end. The revolution he had waited and worked so hard for had finally arrived. He had spread the international socialist word for all of his adult life, and he had been exiled to many countries throughout Europe and lastly to the United States. He was finally on his way home. Money had been raised, and converts and cohorts were in tow. All that was left was to arrive home in Russia.

HALIFAX, NOVA SCOTIA, CANADA

"I hate Trotsky!
I've kept an eye on his activities for some time.
He's Russia's evil genius..."
—Winston Churchill

The coded telegram from the Naval Intelligence Division (NID) was sent to the British naval control officer in Halifax, Captain O.M. Makins. A copy was also sent to the local fortress intelligence officer, Captain A.R. MacCleave. The orders to Halifax said:

"Following are on board KRISTIANIAFJORD and should be taken off retained pending instruction. TROTSKY VOSKOFF GLADNOWSKI MUCHIN and others. These are Russian socialists leaving for purpose of starting revolution against present Russian Government for which

TROTSKY is reported to have 10,000 dollars subscribed by Socialists and Germans."

As the *S.S. Kristianiafjord* sailed closer to Halifax harbour, those aboard were being careful. Journalist William Shepherd stated: "We tore up useless papers because we had heard that the British navy men who inspected all ships, from passengers' watch-fobs to the last chunk of coal, wanted every bit of paper explained." Paranoia reigned supreme, and "Some of us," Shepherd related, "with a German accent were very careful not to express opinions about the war, because the rumor went about that there were certain English chaps on board who sailed on every trip just to listen to what passengers said before they got to Halifax." Every indication suggests that there were indeed at least four British agents aboard the ship. There were signs that one of Trotsky's group was not what they seemed to be as well.

Shepherd said, "We were all rather careful on that run from New York to Halifax." He wrote, "One gloomy, broody, dark-faced youth, who told me that he had renounced Judaism for good and all, said to me: 'I will tell you after we get past the British at Halifax what has happened in my life. It is awful.'" Shepherd, ever the dramatist, said that the "youth," whose age was not given, had "drank many bottles of dark wine in the smoking-room, though he said he had never touched a drop of liquor in his life until three months before." He told Shepherd, "When we have passed Halifax, I shall tell you why I try to be drunk."

Shepherd also said, "Another Russian, a Socialist, declined to say whether or not Russia should take Constantinople—until we had passed Halifax...."

Shepherd said, "The red flags dropped from general sight" as they drew closer to their destination. As the *S.S. Kristianiafjord* sailed into Halifax harbour, Shepherd summed the situation up as he saw it. He stated, "On the dead level, we were a guilty boatload that steamed into Halifax harbor."

On Saturday, 30 March 1917, Captain Makins, along with several sailors from *HMS Devonshire*, boarded the *Kristianiafjord* for what the passengers were told was a "routine inspection." Captain Makins quickly identified those listed in the Admiralty cablegram and subsequently refused the captain of the *S.S. Kristianiafjord* permission to leave Halifax harbour. Two days later, on Tuesday, 1 April 1917, Makins returned to the ship for a more thorough examination of the vessel and its passengers. The visit by the British was a little more eventful this time around.

Trotsky said of his first encounter with the British:

> "…[the] inspection by the British naval authorities, [and] the police officers, who looked through the papers of the Americans, Norwegians, Danes, etc., with only perfunctory formality, subjected us Russians to a direct examination, in the style of old Russian gendarmes, regarding our convictions, political plans, etc. In conformity with good old Russian tradition, I declined to enter into any conversation with them about such matters, having explained to them that I was ready to give them all necessary information establishing my identity, but that my relations to internal Russian politics were not at present under the control of British naval police. "You may have all the information you want to my identity, but nothing else". But this did not prevent the investigating officers…from gathering information about us among other passengers, for instance, from Mr. Fundaminsky, these officers insisting at the same time that I was a "terrible socialist.…

"The whole business was so offensive, so clearly a discrimination against the Russian revolutionaries, in contrast to the treatment accorded other passengers not so unfortunate as to belong to a nation allied to England, that some of the Russians sent a violent protest to the British authorities."

Trotsky said that he "did not join with them because I saw little use in complaining to Beelzebub about Satan." As if he sensed that something was not quite right, he quipped, "But at the time we did not foresee the future."

Meanwhile, William Shepherd, who had boarded the ship in South Brooklyn, New York, had keenly observed a different set of circumstances in Halifax harbour. Contrary to Trotsky's assertions that he and his Russian travelling companions had been singled out for special attention, Shepherd wrote:

"The British Jackies [sailors] attacked the salon first, searching under cushions everywhere in full view of the passengers. As soon as they departed from the salon several persons hid letters addressed to German banks under the cushions, believing the Jackies would not return. The Jackies did return, however; found the letters under the cushions; instituted examination of the passengers; and found the guilty ones."

American journalist and communist Lincoln Steffens remembered that amongst the Russian and Japanese revolutionists aboard, there were also "war messengers, two from Wall Street to Germany and spies and war businessmen...[and] no tourists!" Steffens said:

"At Halifax we and the ship were searched, and we saw good cause for anxiety. The harbor was full of ships, German, Norwegian, Swedish—all sorts of ships that had not got by the search, which was pretty thorough. Having gone through us once and given us the impression that that was the end, having given us time to bring out of hiding whatever we had to conceal, the British searched us again—and again, and yet again. And the British take command and order you about as if they really ruled the waves."

This search went on for two days, and every time the British searched, Shepherd related, "more letters were found under the same cushions. Just when it seemed to somebody of a German psychological cast that the sailors wouldn't be so silly as to search the salon again, they did search it again with good results."

Also on board was a former Russian ambassador to the United States, Andrei Kalpaschnikoff. Kalpaschnikoff wrote in his autobiography, "When the ship came to Halifax the English police, suspecting that there might be among the emigrants some German agents disguised as Bolsheviks, decided to verify carefully the identity of the Russian emigrants. Many of them scarcely spoke any English and someone had to interpret."

Was it mere coincidence that this man with ties to the Czarist regime, and therefore of interest and benefit to the Allies, was on the same ship as a determined group of revolutionaries, led by Trotsky, heading back to Russia?

Interestingly, Kalpaschnikoff said, "I was the only government official and the commander of the port asked me to help him, which I did willingly." Kalpaschnikoff was actually an ex-official in the Czarist government, not a member of the new Provisional government—or was he working for them? He could have been a British plant placed on the ship by MI1(c)'s New York bureau chief William Wiseman. More likely, though, he was an agent of the Czarist secret police organization, the Okhrana. Known for its brutal torture techniques, the Okhrana was created to combat leftist anti-government activities at home and abroad. The reason for Kalpaschnikoff's presence on the *S.S. Kristianiafjord* may become clearer later.

Kalpaschnikoff said, "Among the emigrants questioned in my presence was Trotsky." Shepherd wrote:

> "One morning, a Navy tug came alongside as usual; but this time the Jackies all wore revolvers strapped to their belts. They climbed aboard with unwonted ginger and lined up on the second deck in two grim little rows. Soon word went over the ship that [the] Socialists were being questioned and heckled down in a certain cabin. They went in one at a time to where a British Navy officer sat. Trotsky, the great, went in like any other common Socialist."

Shepherd, a skilled investigative journalist, found out that the Russians "took the grilling well, admitted they were Socialists, and declared themselves proud of it." He added, "Now that we know all the facts, none of us blame that firm-faced young British naval officer at Halifax…Orders are orders. And so the great Trotsky and his five closest companions and worshipers did not go to Russia."

After his second visit to the *S.S. Kristianiafjord*, Captain Makins telegraphed his superiors at Admiralty Headquarters in London. He said:

> "The names given in the cable are not all correct but in any opinion there are six men in the 2nd class…. They are all avowed Socialists, and though professing a desire to help

the new Russian Gov't [sic], might well be in league with German Socialists in America, and quite likely a hindrance to the Government in Russia just at present."

"It is therefore proposed to remove them from the *S.S. Kristianiafjord* on Tuesday morning [April 3, 1917] and hand them over to the military authorities for internment pending further instructions."

"It is proposed to remove also the wife and two boys of Trotsky and make arrangements for their detention pending further instructions."

The morning of Tuesday, 3 April 1917 was a beautiful spring day. The sea was calm as the naval launch from HMS Devonshire, loaded with Captain Makins and a company of armed sailors, moved towards the *S.S. Kristianiafjord*. As the boat pulled alongside the ship, several passengers, according to Andrei Kalpaschnikoff, "all rushed on deck to see what was going to happen." Makins and his armed escort went below deck to the 2nd class quarters, where they found Trotsky and the others. Makins reported to his superiors that:

> "I arrested him…[and] his associates and I had some job, he resisted and as there were aboard about two hundred Russians, Jews, etc., we had quite a lively fight, first in the state room and then on deck. Two man-o-war sailors had a hold on him when he dropped on the floor of the state room screeching 'Bloody Murder' in Russian. He had a head of long hair and when he tried to bite the hand of one of the sailors, I grabbed his hair and at the time I thought I yanked it too hard but I have since wished I had pulled it off…."

William Shepherd said:

"What happened was like a scene in an old sea-tale. Down the ladder to the little tug we saw sailors carrying scarred wooden trunks, the baggage of the Russian outcasts who had been shunted about the earth because of their dream of a Czarless Russia; next a tall, hatless, long-haired youth went down the steps with British Jackies before and behind him. It was a strange sight to see the youth from Grand Street cafes in the hands of pistoled British Jackies. Then came a woman with two children; then two more young men.

"From the deck of the tug men, women, and children looked up and talked, young men shouted, waved their hands, and seemed to be making speeches.

"Then came Trotsky. He fought; six British Jackies patiently, smilingly, carried him; he fought, shouted – not hysterically, but in a slow, dogged, determined way, as if he felt it his duty not to go down peacefully. A British officer went down last, and the last we saw of the tug the British Officers were waving cheery good-byes to the officers of our ship, while some Socialists from another part of the tiny deck, enjoying a Hyde-Parkish freedom of speech which seemed absolutely not to annoy the Jackies, continued to make speeches until out of sight."

Andrei Kalpaschnikoff wrote in his autobiography, "Trotsky and several others were brought out [on deck]. He protested and kicked but was carried down by big strapping seamen who did their work calmly and methodically. As the boat moved away Trotsky shook his fist at the English officers and cursed England."

A mere eight months later, the tables turned, and it was Kalpaschnikoff imprisoned on Trotsky's order for attempting to overthrow the Soviet government. In his autobiography, which was entitled aptly *A Prisoner of Trotsky's,* Kalpaschnikoff wrote, "As I sat in my dirty stuffy little cell I wondered what could be the reason." At the time, "it was strictly forbidden to give any information about me even to my family." He also said, "Trotsky had called me, in one of his speeches, 'the black hand which pressed on the English police to have the honest Bolsheviks arrested on their way home.'"

Kalpaschnikoff finally asked himself, "Could it be his personal vengeance?" Quite possibly, yes. Trotsky never forgave him for the part he played in his arrest and detention in Canada—which, on the surface, seemed to involve more than merely translating for the British in Halifax.

Andrei Kalpaschnikoff escaped from his captivity at the hands of Leon Trotsky and went to America, where he published his autobiography in 1920.

The final word about Trotsky's extraction from the *S.S. Kristianiafjord* came from Trotsky himself. In his autobiography, entitled *My Life* (1930), Trotsky said:

> "...British officers, accompanied by bluejackets, came aboard the CHRISTIANIAFJORD [*S.S. Kristianiafjord*] and demanded, in the name of the local admiral, that I, my family, and five other passengers leave the boat. We were assured that the whole incident would be cleared up in Halifax. We declared that the order was illegal and refused to obey, whereupon armed bluejackets pounced on us, and amid shouts of 'shame' from a large part of the passengers, carried us bodily

to a naval cutter, which delivered us in Halifax under the convoy of a cruiser. While a group of sailors were holding me fast, my older boy ran to help me and struck an officer with his little fist. 'Shall I hit him again, Papa?' He was eleven then and it was his first lesson in British democracy."

While this event played out aboard the *S.S. Kristianiafjord*, Lincoln Steffens noticed that a couple of the passengers seemed to be avoiding detention and scrutiny. He said:

"[The British] held us for a week or more [in Halifax harbour], an anxious week during which everybody worried except the Wall Street messengers to Germany. They, with their trunk load of 'bonds, etc.' [we heard], were not inconvenienced. I asked one of them afterward, in a warm moment of confidence, how they got by, they of all people.

"'Oh,' it was explained, 'when you are in the business you study it and you fix it.'"

Then Steffens made an interesting observation:

"So all but the professional guilty are in danger from the secret service as from any other police. War intensifies everything; it doesn't change anything. Suspicion, for example, becomes patriotic and the grafters, patriots, and the reds, not the crooks and traitors, are the victims. The German box of 'bonds,' valuables, and information got by Halifax, but Trotsky was taken off and held for weeks—this though the United States recognized the new revolutionary Russian government, and the British had not yet decided not to."

Finally, Steffens stated:

"After Halifax that Swedish ship steamed far to the north, nearly to Iceland, and came darkened into the war zone, where the German and the British ships were fighting. The passengers sat up one night, singing, drinking, playing boisterously—frightened—and the ship's officers fanned the fright. But the spies and the smugglers smiled, and the captain's eyes twinkled. Somehow I got the impression that there was some bunk about it all. That ship's passage across the war front was 'fixed' with both sides, and the risk was only of an accident; some warship might collide with us or shoot without inquiry. We got safely across, saw sturdy Norway with its arctic evening."

Makins proceeded with Trotsky and the other eight taken from the *S.S. Kristianiafjord* to the Halifax Citadel (or as it is formally known, Fort George) for further interrogation. The fourth citadel, completed in 1856 after twenty-eight years of construction, was the centerpiece of the Halifax Defence Complex. This included several forts, batteries, and redoubts, as well as a dockyard created to defend Great Britain's only year-round deep-water naval port in the North Atlantic.

While garrisoned by the Canadian Army since 1906, the British Navy was still master of the port, as Trotsky and his entourage were quick to find out. As the staging point for all convoys heading from Canada to Great Britain, and considering Canada's still fledgling navy, it was only logical that Great Britain would assume control over the port and all matters pertaining to it, such as intelligence.

After a lengthy session with Makins and the local fortress intelligence officer, Captain A.R. MacCleave, it was decided that

Trotsky and his five male companions would be taken by train to the Amherst Prisoner of War Internment Camp. The camp was ninety miles west, situated on the Nova Scotia and New Brunswick border. Trotsky would write in his autobiography, *My Life* (1930), that:

> "The British authorities, according to the admission of their own officers had not the slightest doubts about my identity or of the identity of the others whom they detained. It was clear, that we were detained as socialists, imaginary or real ones, that is, as opponents to war.... At Halifax not only was nothing 'explained' to us, but they even refused to call the local Russian Consul, assuring us that there was a Russian Consul at the place to which we were brought. This assurance proved to be false as well as all the other assurances of the British secret police, who in their methods and morals stand entirely on the same level as the old Russian 'Okhrana.'"

This still left British authorities with the delicate question of what to do with Trotsky's wife and two young sons, Lev and Sergei. The Salvation Army and the Home of the Good Shepherd were considered but deemed unacceptable because children were not permitted to stay in these facilities. It was subsequently decided that Natalya Sedova and her two sons would be lodged in the home of David Horowetz, the official Russian interpreter in Halifax, who was present at the interrogation proceedings at the Halifax Citadel.

Natalya Sedova
(https://spartacus-educational.com/Natalia_Sedova.htm)

Leon Trotsky (Wikimedia Commons)

AMHERST, NOVA SCOTIA

On 3 April 1917, the six Russian men taken from the *S.S. Kristianiafjord*, all avowed Socialists, were transferred by rail and began twenty-six days of incarceration at the Amherst Prisoner of War Internment Camp in Amherst, Nova Scotia. During their initial processing, Leon Bronstein Trotsky was listed as prisoner number 1098, age thirty-seven, whose occupation was that of a journalist.

Trotsky's "right-hand man" at *Novy Mir* was twenty-seven-year-old journalist Grigori Chudnovski, who was with Trotsky in Paris and was associated with Alexander Parvus, the Russo-Germanic socialist "Merchant of Revolution." Parvus was a millionaire, Russian socialist, and arms dealer. He became a German/British agent to disrupt Czarist Russia's war effort. In late 1916, Parvus had to convince Trotsky that going to the United States was in the best interest of the coming revolution.

Gregori Chudnovski's relationship to Trotsky remained close. He was a member of the RSDRP from 1905, of the Mezhraionka group from May 1917, and of the 'Bolshevik Party' from July. As well, he was a prominent member of the Bolsheviks' Military Organization and the Petrograd Soviet's Military Revolutionary Committee. He participated in the capture of the Winter Palace and arrest of the Provisional Government. He died in the Ukraine during the Civil War. In Amherst, in April 1917, Chudnovski was Amherst prisoner number 1099.

Next was Liebe Fishelev, (listed as Lieke Fisheleff on his internment documents). He was a thirty-six-year-old journalist who wrote for *Freie Arbeiter Stimme*, a New York-based Jewish anarchist newspaper. Fishelev had spent several years in Paris prior to coming to America in 1914, after which he lived in New York. He was prisoner number 1100.

Thirty-two-year-old Konstantin Romanchenko and twenty-seven-year-old Nikita Muchin left Russia in 1913. Precious little is known of their fate after leaving Amherst, but anomalies arose. They were prisoner numbers 1102 and 1101 respectively.

Last was thirty-one-year-old watchmaker Grigori Melnitchanski. He came from the same province as Trotsky in southern Russia and had been in New York since 1910. While connected to *Novy Mir* in some unknown way, he later commanded an important position within the Comintern (short for the Communist International), an international communist organization that advocated world communism. In a note to the American secretary of state in 1920, a British general said that Melnitchanski was a Comintern delegate who "directs all work connected with American communism." He was also connected to the Soviet Textile Trust and the Soviet-American trading firm Amtorg. Melnitchanski was prisoner number 1097.

Immediately upon their arrival in Amherst, the six Russians were again cross-examined. It was the duty of the camp's second-in-command, Captain John Frederick Carman Wightman, a twenty-three-year-old civil engineering student from Mount Allison University. As a member of the Canadian Officer Training Corps (C.O.T.C.), Wightman jumped at the chance to serve "King and Country" when he graduated from the C.O.T.C. and Mount Allison on 26 May 1915. Within a week, he had signed up and was immediately designated a captain, yet because of a lingering health problem, he was deemed unfit for overseas duty. By mid-July 1915, he was assigned to the prisoner of war camp in Amherst as a platoon commander until his promotion to Adjutant in March 1916.

Every prisoner was required to have an Army Form IB-L filled out, which detailed all of their pertinent personal particulars. Up to this point, Trotsky had not been told the true nature of his incarceration. Trotsky informed Captain Wightman that he was a Russian citizen travelling on a valid Russian passport. When it came time to be fingerprinted, Trotsky simply refused.

"I had to forcibly take his fingerprints," Captain Wightman said. "I had a sergeant hold him, then I took his hands, put them on the ink pad and put them on the form." When asked if Trotsky reacted in any way to the forcible fingerprinting, Wightman said that he began yelling and "he became a little violent. Then there was no trouble."

Trotsky told a different tale. He said:

> "In the office [in Amherst], we were put through an examination the likes of which I had never before experienced... in my confinement in the fortress of Peter and Paul. For the stripping and feeling of our bodies by gendarmes was done at the fortress in private, with no one else present, but here, our democratic allies subjected us to this impudent horseplay in the presence of a dozen men. And those

commanding scoundrels who were in charge of this procedure, well knew that we were Russian socialists who are returning to their country that was set free by revolution."

In another account, Trotsky added, "I can remember Sergeant Olsen, a Swedish-Canadian with a red head of the criminal-police type, who was the leader of the search." Trotsky said, "The *canaille* [a derogatory term used to refer to the common people] who had arranged all this from a distance knew well enough that we were irreproachable Russian revolutionaries returning to our country, liberated by the revolution."

Guards at the Amherst Internment Camp, WW I. (Author's Collection)

"IRREPROACHABLE RUSSIAN REVOLUTIONARIES"

To many people, the Russian prisoners were the exact antithesis of "irreproachable." The first person to hold this view in Amherst was internment camp commandant Colonel Arthur Henry Morris. He was Trotsky's jailer for twenty-six days. Morris was the classic Victorian officer. Born in 1861 on the Isle of Wight, he was the son of Reverend Henry Morris and Eliza Jemima Morris. Educated at King's College Canterbury, Morris thereafter received a commission with the Royal Irish Regiment in 1883 after a short period with the Yorkshire Artillery Militia. Before long, he saw action in the Sudan Expedition for the relief of General Gordon in 1884 and 1885, after which he received medal with clasp and the bronze star. From 1885 to 1887, he served in the Burmese War, as well as the Expedition against the Red Karens under Brigadier-General Sir Henry Collett. This time, he received a medal with two clasps and was mentioned in despatches. Next, he served as Chief Transport Officer to the Chin Lushai Expedition of 1889 to 1890 under Brigadier-General Sir W.P. Symons, where he was mentioned in despatches, thanked by the Government of India, and created a Companion of the Distinguished Service Order (DSO).

In 1891, Morris was promoted to Captain. From 1899 to 1904, he was in West Africa as Chief Commissioner of the Northern Territories of the Gold Coast, a territory which spanned over forty thousand square miles. In 1900, after being promoted to Major, Morris twice led expeditions against the Northern Territories, where he was twice mentioned in despatches. During the Ashanti Uprisings of 1900, Morris commanded a column of soldiers, which forced its way into the city of Kumasi, in present-day Ghana. During the march, Morris was severely wounded in the groin, yet he continued to lead his men, despite "intervals of unconsciousness," by being carried by cart. Even while injured, he commanded the garrison which defended the British governor of the territory, Sir Frederick Mitchell Hodgson, and the city of Kumasi during the siege by the Ashanti. Finally, he successfully led the group, which included the governor and his wife, out of Kumasi in a race against twelve thousand Ashanti warriors to make it to the British Garrison at Accra, which was two hundred and fifty kilometers away.

He continued his career by becoming a Companion of the Most Distinguished Order of Saint Michael and Saint George (CMG) in 1904 for his service in Burma and on the Gold Coast during the Ashanti Uprising of 1900. After the uprising, Morris received medal with clasp and Brevet of Lieutenant Colonel. In 1902, he married Dorothy Mary Wilkie, and in 1908, they celebrated the birth of their only child, John Henry Morris. In November of 1908, he became a full colonel, and from 1908 to 1913, he commanded the Duke of

York's Royal Military School in Dover. In July 1913, he retired from the British Army after thirty years of service.

Morris and his family emigrated to Canada in 1914. His adjutant said sixty years later that Morris wanted to be a farmer.

In the summer of 1915, shortly after the opening of the Amherst Internment Camp, a riot occurred. One prisoner was killed and four were injured. A court of inquiry was held, and it was recommended that the officer commanding the Amherst Camp, Major G.R. Oulton, be relieved of his duties since discipline was severely lacking amongst his troops.

In Sackville, New Brunswick, attempting to live the life of a gentleman farmer, was Morris, who had thirty years' experience in the British Imperial Army and had led men in difficult circumstances. Commanding a prisoner of war camp came as second nature to Morris, who was steeped in the militaristic tradition where discipline had to be observed and maintained. This was the man that Leon Trotsky and his cohorts were up against in the Amherst Prisoner of War Internment Camp in April 1917.

The next morning, on 4 April, Trotsky and Morris finally met.

After that first meeting, Trotsky said that Morris, "in answer to our repeated demands and protests, [told] us the official reason for the arrest. 'You are dangerous to the present Russian Government.'" Trotsky felt that Morris was "obviously not a man of eloquence," and that he had "worn an air of rather suspicious excitement since early morning."

Trotsky explained to the Colonel that they had received their Russian passports from "agents" of the current Russian Government in New York. Morris, who never minced words and spoke with such economy that each word spoken seemed to cost a small fortune, told Trotsky and his compatriots that they "were dangerous to the allies in general." Trotsky lamented the fact that no official documents were produced with regards to their detention. Morris, according to Trotsky, "added a personal remark that, as political emigrants, who had been obliged to leave their own country for some reason, we should not be surprised at what was happening to us now."

"The Russian revolution did not exist for this man," Trotsky said of Colonel Morris. The socialist émigrés attempted to enlighten the colonel on how "the Czar's ministers, who made political emigrants of us, were themselves in prison now, but this was too complex for the commandant, who had made his career in the British Colonies…."

In a letter addressed to the Russian Foreign Minister, written while sailing back to Russia directly after release from Amherst, Trotsky wrote about Morris:

"For characterizing this worthy representative of ruling Britain it is sufficient to state, that one of his favorite expressions addressed to disobedient or disrespectful prisoners was: 'If I only had you on the South African coast.' If it can be said that style is the man, then it can be said that this style—that is, this system, is the British colonial system…For Colonel Morris we were political emigrants, rebels against legal authorities and therefore a camp for war prisoners was the most natural place for us to live in."

NEW YORK

During his three months in New York at the beginning of 1917, Trotsky was enveloped in an intrigue so large, it could make a person's head spin. There were spies and double agents from every combatant country in the war in the largest city in North America. They were all doing everything possible to give their nation (and often giving themselves advantages, whether monetary or strategic) a leg up on their adversary. As outlined earlier, spies were plentiful on both sides. Sidney Reilly, the "Ace of Spies," played Russia off against Britain, Germany, and the United States, often in whatever combination suited his situation at the time.

There was also Sir William Wiseman, head of Section V of MI1c, precursor to MI6, who controlled the whole affair from New York under the pretence of being a member of Sir Winston Churchill's Ministry of Munitions. This was a pretence for his duplicitous dealings on behalf of the Allied war effort, often to the exclusion of other Allied countries and especially other British and Allied intelligence services. Wiseman used the likes of Sidney Reilly (who was Czarist by nature) and his cabal, which included both Alexander and Gregory Weinstein in New York. While Alexander Weinstein was a Russian royalist, his brother Gregory was the financial manager of *Novy Mir*, the socialist newspaper Trotsky wrote for while in Gotham.

There was also Abram Zhivotovski, a Bolshevik-leaning Russian with deep connections to many European banks. He was suspected of being an arms dealer who often diverted arms and munitions to Germany. He also happened to be Trotsky's uncle.

British spymaster Sir William Wiseman knew that the Czar's days were numbered and that he needed to manage the fallout if Russia left the war. If Russia exited the war, then the Allies would face an uncertain future at a critical time. The situation needed to be managed from inside of Russia.

Germany had already been stirring the pot by financing Vladimir Lenin's return to Russia in exchange for cooperation and withdrawal from the war. It was not above Wiseman to use Trotsky as a counterbalance against Germany, whether Trotsky wanted too or not. And it was not above Leon Trotsky to take money from fellow Czarist-hating financier Jacob Schiff. The issue of the ten thousand dollars of German money is more than likely a low-ball estimate. The Germans would most definitely have financed Trotsky if they lavishly financed Lenin. Trotsky was pragmatic, as was Wiseman, and it was to their mutual benefit if Russia stayed in the war in exchange for massive amounts of money, farm tractors, cars, and other technologies to help an incredibly archaic and feudal-like Russia.

Trotsky didn't care for the war, the Germans, the British, or the Americans. He only cared about the revolution. To him, the revolution had to move into Germany and continue across Europe and internationally, and if he had to beg, borrow or steal, then so be it. The revolution must succeed.

LETTING THE WORLD KNOW

After the removal of Trotsky and the others from the *S.S. Kristianiafjord,* journalist Lincoln Steffens and the remaining radicals aboard drafted a telegram. According to Charles Crane, the telegram was sent to various revolutionaries in New York, thus raising the alarm that their comrades had been detained. It seems unlikely that this telegram ever left Halifax, considering wartime censorship, if Steffens ever sent it to begin with. He would hardly wish to interject himself into an international incident when his benefactor, Charles Crane, was paying his way.

The news that Trotsky and company had been detained eventually made its way to New York via a letter sent to Gregory Weinstein at the offices of *Novy Mir* by one of the internees, Grigorii Chudnovskii. In his letter, he wrote:

> "The British Military Authorities found that we, a group of Russian Socialists, are dangerous to the cause of the Allies.

> They took us off the ship and sent us to an internment camp for Prisoners of War in Amherst. We protested and refused to leave, but in spite of all they dragged us off by force. We sent telegrams to the Russian Consul in Halifax and Montreal, to the Russian Minister for Foreign Affairs, and the Russian Minister of Justice, the Vice President of the Deputation, Committee of Workers and Soldiers, Tchkeidze, to the New York 'Call' and some private people. We do not know whether the telegrams arrived. They left us without clothes and even took away our towels and handkerchiefs. Direct material help is necessary. It is also necessary to take steps to set us free."

Weinstein spread the news amongst as many newspapers as possible, both socialist and non-socialist. News of Trotsky's detainment appeared in *The New York Times* on 11 April 1917. The newspaper said, "One of the prisoners wrote to a friend in New York, who gave out the letter for publication yesterday." Any hopes that this episode would remain quiet faded with the publication of Trotsky's incarceration.

On the day after their arrival at Amherst, 4 April, the Russian consul at Montreal received a telegram from the six Russian socialists at Amherst, deploring Consul General Lichatchoff to assist them in any way possible. Trotsky and the others stated in the telegram that:

> "We undersigned political refugees after declaration of amnesty by present Russian Government returning via Norway to our country with passports issued Russian consul General New York are arrested Halifax on board 'Kristiania.' Held by British military authorities without

any cause and reason and interned internment station Amherst together with German prisoners of war. We energetically protest against such unprecedented act and demand your immediate intervention to protect our interests of Russian citizens and dignity of government which you represent.

Signed trotsky melnitchaniny fishieff ishoodnouski muchin konstantin romanchenka"

Joseph Pope, the Canadian undersecretary of state for external affairs, replying to a query about the matter by the Russian Consul General a few days later, stated that, "I am informed that this action was taken at the request of the Admiralty; the persons arrested being Russian Socialists animated with the purpose of starting revolution against the present Russian Government." This seemed to be the end of the matter as far as the consul general was concerned.

In a letter written to Russian Foreign Minister Mikhail Tereshchenko while aboard the Danish ship *S.S. Hellig Olav* after his release from detention in Amherst, Trotsky admitted that he had no contact with the Russian government. He had, in fact, been in contact with the Russian consul general in Montreal.

Trotsky, in the same paragraph, said that all further attempts to communicate with the Russian government were thwarted, nor were they even allowed to communicate with the consul general again by the authorities at Amherst. He also noted that the Russian consul general never communicated with them again after their first telegram. Trotsky said, "British-Canadian authorities used every means to cut us off from the Russian government and its agents." In fact, as soon as the consul general received the telegram from

Amherst, he sent one to the provisional government in Petrograd, as well as an inquiry to Joseph Pope about the matter.

Lichatchoff also sent a telegram to the chief of the Canadian military general staff, Lieutenant General Sir Willoughby Garnons Gwatkin. He forwarded the letter to the director of internment operations, Major-General Sir William Otter, who was a battle-hardened veteran of the Fenian raids, the Northwest Rebellion, and the Boer War. In his missive to Otter, Gwatkin said of the detainment of Trotsky and his entourage, "in this connection, [I] have to inform you of the receipt of a long telegram yesterday from the Russian Consul General, Montreal, protesting against the arrest of these men as they were in possession of passports issued by the Russian Consul General, New York, U.S.A."

Otter's reply was that these men were detained "on suspicion of being German," and would only be freed upon ample proof of the nationality and loyalty to the Allies.

The Russian Consul General in Montreal availed himself at the same time to send a similar missive to Otter. The head of Internment Operations informed Gwatkin that he wrote to the Russian Consul General in Montreal, stating:

> "In this connection I have to inform you of the receipt of a long telegram yesterday from the Russian Consul General, Montreal, protesting against the arrest of these men as they were in possession of passports issued by the Russian Consul General, New York, U.S.A.
>
> "To this I replied that these men were interned by the naval authorities at Halifax on suspicion of being Germans, they cannot be released unless upon definite proof of their nationality and loyalty to the allies."

One person aligned with Trotsky and the Russo-Jewish socialist cabal in New York also complained directly to Canadian authorities about the detention of the Russian socialists in Amherst. Nicholas Aleinikoff, a lawyer from New York, who was born in the Ukraine, like Trotsky, in 1861. Because of the Russian pogroms of the early 1880s, two reform-minded groups of Russian Jews decided to leave Russia. One of these groups went to Palestine (called BILU or "Let the house of Jacob go") and the other (Am Olam, meaning "Eternal People") journeyed to the United States. Aleinikoff joined the latter group and left for America in 1882, where he organized the Am Olam radical communal Jewish colony in New York. From there, Am Olam branched out to Connecticut, Louisiana, North Dakota, California, and Oregon. They called their new settlement New Odessa.

Aleinikoff remained in New York, where he became prominent amongst New York's working-class Jewish organizations. He somehow became entwined with various anarchist groups and had to defend himself when he was linked to anarchist assassin Alexander Berkman. Berkman, who was in league with well-known Anarchist Emma Goldman (who in 1917 would be quite impressed with Leon Trotsky), attempted to kill industrialist Henry Clay Frick at the Carnegie Steel Company offices in Homestead, Pennsylvania. On 23 July 1892, seventeen days after Frick hired three hundred Pinkerton thugs to dismantle a strike and a gun battle resulted in nine union workers and seven Pinkertons killed, Berkman's attempt to kill Frick failed. He was captured at the scene.

In the search for accomplices—namely Emma Goldman and Berkman's cousin Modest Aronstam—police checked "all the usual suspects." Eventually, this brought them to Aleinikoff, who was, according to the 26 July 1892 issue of *The New York Times*, "the leader of the Russian Revolution Party in this city."

Aleinikoff vehemently denied knowing Berkman and told the reporter, "I do not understand why I should be dragged into this affair at all. True enough, I am in sympathy with revolutionary methods in Russia. It is the people's only recourse there, but in America, never. Here we have free institutions and a free press, and I would be first among any body of men to deprecate violent and high-handed actions by Anarchists or anyone."

In this vein, a great deal of revolutionary activity occurred in New York from the 1880s up until 1917. Aleinikoff, a prominent lawyer in the Russo-Jewish community of the city, was inextricably linked to the likes of Sidney Reilly, Gregory Weinstein, and Dr. Nikolai Kuznetsov, who was an automobile specialist and instructor at the Petrograd Military Institute. Yet Aleinikoff's brother Benjamin was an anarchist. While it is unknown if he had ties to Berkman, he certainly had ties to the Zhivotovskii clan, who were related to Trotsky.

And of course, Aleinikoff knew Trotsky himself from the latter's time in New York. Both their names appear on a document entitled "Socialists of City Will Fight War Measures," dated 4 March 1917. Published in *The New York Call*, it stated, "In the event of a war declaration, New York City Socialists will use every endeavor to hasten the return of peace, to oppose the war policies of the government...."

When Aleinikoff heard of Trotsky's detention in Canada, he penned a letter to Canada's deputy postmaster general. This was on 10 April, a full day before *The New York Times* article announced Trotsky's incarceration to the world. Aleinikoff most likely heard about it from insiders at *Novy Mir*, but in his wire to R.M. Coulter in Ottawa, he informed him that, "Russian political exiles returning to Russia detained Halifax, interned Amherst camp. Kindly investigate and advise cause of the detention and names of all detained. Trust as champions of freedom you will intercede on their behalf. Nicholas Aleinikoff." And as a social courtesy, he asked that Canada's deputy postmaster general should "Please wire collect."

The next day, 11 April 1917, Coulter replied to Aleinikoff. He told him that Trotsky and the others were indeed in the Amherst internment camp, and they were accused of using propaganda against the provisional government of Russia and being "agents of Germany." The Deputy Postmaster General told Aleinikoff that the group "are not what they represent themselves to be" and that they were detained by the British and not the Canadians. Coulter assured the American lawyer that they would be treated well, and he would forward any pertinent information "in their favour." The Canadian Postal Service paid for the telegram.

Another man, Arthur Wolf of New York City, also sent a telegram, this time collect, to Coulter on behalf of the Russian detainees.

Coulter sent a letter to Major General Gwatkin, saying, "These men have been hostile to Russia because of the way the Jews have been treated, and are now strongly in favour of the present Administration, so far as I know. Both are reputable men, and I am sending their telegrams to you for what they may be worth, and so that you may represent them to the English authorities if you deem it wise."

Aleinikoff replied, thanking Coulter for his intervention and "for the interest you have taken in the fate of the Russian Political Exile…You know me, esteemed Dr. Coulter, and you also know my devotion to the cause of Russian freedom…Happily I know Mr. Trotsky, Mr. Melnichahnsky, and Mr. Chudnowsky…intimately."

This missive, too, was forwarded to Gwatkin with an added note stating that he (Coulter) knew Aleinikoff "in connection with Departmental action on United States papers in the Russian language" and that Aleinikoff "was working on the same lines as Mr. Wolf…who was an escaped prisoner from Siberia."

Coulter all but admitted that Aleinikoff and Wolf were working as informants for the Canadian postal department when it came to Russian language publications in the United States, which included *Novy Mir*. Canada also had significant immigrant Russian socialist populations in Toronto and Vancouver that needed tending, and it would have been prudent for eyes to be kept on radical publications entering Canada.

On 5 April 1917, one day before the American Congress declared war on Germany and the rest of the Central Powers, the British Foreign Office sent a note to their ambassador in Petrograd, Sir George Buchanan:

> "Russian socialists, Trotsky, Voshoff, Gladnowski, Mucher, and two others have been removed from S.S. "Christianiafjord" at Halifax homeward bound from New York.
>
> "We understand that Trotsky is leader of a movement subsidized by Socialists and Germany, to upset present Russian Government.
>
> "They are being detained for the present. Please enquire of Minister of Foreign Affairs whether he considers these men should be allowed to proceed."

The reply from the Russian Foreign Minister, Pavel Milyukov, who was an avowed adversary of Trotsky's, was presented to Buchanan on 9 April. Buchanan, in a telegram to the British Foreign Office, said:

> "[The Russian] Minister of Foreign Affairs said that if socialists were detained here extremists would be sure to hear

of it and Government would eventually be obliged to allow them to proceed. He would therefore prefer they should be allowed to proceed at once."

The Russian Minister of Justice at this time was Alexander Kerensky, and there is evidence that he was, along with Lenin (and quite possibly Trotsky), in the paid service of the Germans. It is quite possible he ordered Trotsky's release when news of their incarceration came across his desk.

Milyukov was pro-British, pro-war, and anti-Trotsky. On 10 April, he seemed to have won this tug-of-war (he lost the next one on 18 April and subsequently resigned on his insistence that Russia continue with the war). The British Foreign Office received another telegram on the aforementioned date, saying:

> "[The Russian] Minister of Foreign Affairs [Milyukov] said after consulting the Minister of Justice [Kerensky] he thought that before allowing…[the] anarchists …to proceed it would be better were His Majesty's Government to furnish Russian Government with further details respecting them."

Meanwhile, the Bolshevik newspaper *Pravda*, at Lenin's urging, stated, "Can one even for a moment believe the trustworthiness of the statement that Trotsky, chairman of the Soviet of Workers delegates in St. Petersburg in 1905—a revolutionary who has sacrificed years to a dis-interested service of revolution—that this man had anything to do with a scheme subsidized by the German government?"

The *Pravda* article added, "Six men dragged Comrade Trotsky away by his legs and arms, all in the name of friendship for the Provisional Russian government."

Wiseman, as head of MI1c in New York, was trying to "guide the storm" of Russia's participation in the war in light of the revolution. Trotsky most likely accepted money from Germany; from New York-based German American Jewish financier Jacob Schiff; as well as the British. Everyone had their conditions of acceptance without doubt. Yet Britain ruled the seas and as is often said, "He who holds the gold holds the power." Wiseman admitted that he had been in contact with "anarchist revolutionary socialists" in New York and had been uplifting their pacifistic tendencies with a steady stream of funds and a lot of arm-twisting to contact their brethren in Russia and encourage them to keep fighting.

What separated Trotsky from Lenin was that Trotsky was an international socialist and Lenin was not. Trotsky wanted the revolution to occur simultaneously across Europe, and a separate peace with Germany would not allow this to happen. This was Wiseman's "Ace in the hole," or so he thought. Prima facie evidence suggests that Trotsky and Wiseman (or at least his minion, Norman Thwaites) were known to each other through Trotsky's efforts to receive a British Transit Visa, which was needed to sail across the Atlantic Ocean. It may have been the price of admission to the budding Russian revolution, which Trotsky was so eager to gain admittance to.

When Trotsky showed even the slightest amount of recalcitrance, the British were more than willing to incarcerate him and set him straight by realigning his outlook a bit. So, Trotsky settled in for his brief sojourn in an internment camp in Canada.

SETTLING IN

Immediately after their "check-in," the internal police of the internment camp issued the six Russians with blankets and bunk assignments. Since they were not considered first-class prisoners, a designation reserved solely for German and other Central Power officers and civilian professionals, they resided amongst the other seven hundred prisoners.

Trotsky was less than impressed.

"The military camp in Amherst," he recalled the next year, "is located in an old building of a foundry. The bunks for sleeping are put up in three tiers, and two rows deep on each side. Under these conditions there lived eight hundred men."

Prisoners from the Amherst Internment Camp, World War I. (Author's Collection)

In April 1915, the Amherst camp opened and began accepting its first prisoners. The preparations to get the camp ready for use were done on budget, quickly and without concern for the bare minimum of consideration for the prisoner's comfort. The local newspaper, *The Amherst Daily News,* reported that in each bunk were "straw stuffed mattresses…with heavy blankets which will afford all the greatest amount of comfort." The tabloid said:

> "Incommodity in one way alone, awaits these prisoners. The Malleable (Iron Foundry) is extremely dusty. Year after year, the beams in all departments of the former plant have been collecting dust, and in spots this dust is two inches deep. The work of preparation has brought the dust to the floor in great quantities.

> "With six hundred men moving about the building especially in their dining room, more dust will surely fall. Cleanliness is a virtue, there is no doubt but that the Austrians and Germans are willing to practise it. Outside of the dust no other cause for complaint can be found."

Amherst Internment Camp, Christmas 1916. (Library and Archives Canada—C014104)

In 1917, the building, according to Trotsky, was "unspeakably dirty and neglected." Little had changed in two years regarding the cleanliness and livability of the structure. He said, "You can imagine…the atmosphere in this sleeping place at night. Among the prisoners, in spite of the heroic efforts they made for their physical and moral preservation, there were five insane men. We slept and ate in the same room with these madmen."

Later, he said, "The air in this improvised dormitory at night can be imagined. Men hopelessly dogged the passages, elbowed their way through, lay down or got up, played cards or chess. Many of them practised crafts, some with extraordinary skill." In 1930, years after his exile from Russia, Trotsky spoke fondly of those crafts. Speaking as if one day he would return to Russia, he said, "I still have, stored in Moscow, some things made by Amherst prisoners."

Trotsky said that of the eight hundred prisoners within the wires of the Amherst camp:

"Perhaps five hundred were sailors from German boats sunk by the British; about two hundred were workers caught by the war in Canada, and a hundred more were officers and civilian prisoners of the bourgeois class. Our relations with the German prisoners became clearly defined according to their reaction to the fact that we had been arrested as revolutionary socialists. The officers and petty officers, whose quarters were behind a wooden partition, immediately set us down as enemies, the rank-and-file, on the other hand, surrounded us with an ever increasing friendliness."

It would be that "ever increasing friendliness" that defined Trotsky's sojourn in Amherst.

German officers from Kaiser Wilhelm der Grosse at Amherst Internment Camp, World War I. (Author's Collection)

Canada had incarcerated over eight thousand and five hundred people in their prison camp system during World War I, most of which were Ukrainian-born immigrants lured to Canada with the promise of a better life. The Amherst camp was the country's largest facility of its kind and housed mostly military prisoners, with about twenty-five percent being "enemy aliens."

FRICTION

Trotsky and his fellow Russians became instant celebrities from the first moment that they began to co-mingle with the main prison population in Amherst. He wasted no time spreading the revolutionary word to the prisoners.

Captain F.C. Wightman recalled in an interview conducted in the mid-1970s that from the beginning, Trotsky had been a trouble-maker. "When he got up the first morning… he decided that he was going to convert a lot of Germans into Communists and he did a good job of it…He talked morning, noon, and night; there were meetings [going] on all the time," Wightman recalled.

The prisoners at Amherst were more than receptive of Trotsky's rhetoric. It was a diversion from the monotonous lifestyle most had been experiencing for the previous two years.

Fluent in German (some stated he was more fluent in German than Russian) and thoroughly enraged by the treatment accorded him by his British and Canadian captors, Trotsky's virulent and bombastic oratory never ceased.

> "The rank-and-file surrounded us with a ring of sympathy...The whole month I was there was like one continuous mass-meeting. I told the prisoners about the Russian revolution, about Liebknecht, about Lenin, and about the causes of the collapse of the old International, and the intervention of the United States in the war. Besides these speeches, we had constant group discussions. Our friendship grew warmer every day...The sailors did everything they could to make our life easier, and it was only by constant protests that I kept my right to stand in line for dinner and to do my share of the compulsory work of sweeping the floors, peeling potatoes, washing crockery, and cleaning the common lavatory..."

Trotsky said, "By their attitudes, one could class the rank-and-file of the prisoners in two groups: those who said, "No more of that, we must end it once and for all"—they were the ones who had dreams of coming out into the streets and squares—and those others who said, "What have they to do with me? No, they won't get me again."

Trotsky's warm affection for the common prisoner was evident; his disdain for their officers was equally apparent. Sardonically, Trotsky stated that "relations between the rank-and-file and the officers, some of whom, even in prison, were keeping a sort of conduct-book for their men, were hostile." Trotsky said that the "officers ended by complaining to the camp commander, Colonel Morris, about my anti-patriotic propaganda. The British colonel instantly sided with the Hohenzollern [the name given to the German royal family] patriots and forbade me to make any more speeches."

The internment camp provided the prisoners with one daily newspaper, *The Halifax Chronicle Herald,* but few of the German prisoners could read it because it was written in English. Trotsky took it upon himself to become the official translator for the prisoners even though his English was not that good. He laid the paper out on a large table and translated the text, adding his own revolutionary commentary.

"We had constant group discussions. Our friendship grew warmer every day," Trotsky recalled in his biography.

He soon had quite a large following amongst the rank-and-file prisoners. The guards at the Amherst internment camp even found Trotsky fascinating. Captain Wightman said, "He was a man who, when he looked at you, seemed to hypnotize you."

Surprisingly, it was not the Canadian authorities in the camp who felt threatened by Trotsky's constant pot-stirring. It was, as Trotsky mentioned, the German officers. Class distinctions and military authority did not end at the entrance gates of the prison camp. It came right through the gate with the first prisoners in April 1915.

Wightman said, "The German officers and their men—that was one thing I'll never forget—never bothered with their men. The officers never, at any stage, mixed with their men. I don't know if they ever even spoke to them. They were a race apart...the class lines were very rigid." Wightman said that the regular sailor "would have to be paraded. The officers...never mingled with the men; they lived apart, they ate apart."

Trotsky was instigating revolution amongst the German sailors. He went to great pains to tell them that the Russian soldier had revolted against the Czar and overthrew him. He told them that they could do the same and overthrow the German Kaiser and get rid of the rest of the capitalist cabal in Germany. All they had to do was act.

A short time after Trotsky's arrival, the patriotic, Kaiser-loving German officers began to feel alienated from their men and feared for their own safety. Wightman recalled:

> "This man, Trotsky, had upset the whole atmosphere of the camp and [the German officers] complained to the Colonel that this man should be restrained from acting that way and they were prisoners themselves...They were afraid that he was going to convert the ordinary rank-and-file of these sailors into communists who might in turn kill their own officers. But they were scared and they complained to the Colonel, so the Colonel had to do something."

And Morris did, in fact, do something.

Captain Wightman said, "Trotsky was paraded with armed guards with their bayonets fixed. I still remember that so well. [He was brought] before the Colonel, and of course Trotsky could speak English just as well as you or I, and the Colonel lashed at him and told him that he'd had complaints about him and that propaganda of his and that it had to stop."

The Victorian military officer who had spent most of his career abroad in various British colonies, following strict protocols with little or no humor, was faced with this revolutionary agitator who was upsetting the social order of the camp. Wightman calmly summed up the prevailing feeling at the time by saying, "We didn't want him starting up trouble."

Indeed.

Trotsky's personality and his great dislike of the British combined to make the situation only more volatile. Wightman recalled, "Trotsky...pretty near lost his life" that day. In the course of his dressing down by Morris, "Trotsky...called the Colonel a liar."

According to Captain Wightman:

> "Amongst the escort happened to be a man who had been badly wounded overseas by the Germans and eventually had been sent home; been in hospital and had recovered enough that he had been assigned to duty at the camp as a guard...As soon as he had heard that Trotsky had called the Colonel a liar, well he just took his rifle, that had its bayonet fixed, and was going to shove the bayonet right through Mr. Trotsky. And he would have if there had not been the Sergeant [of the Guard] alongside of him who had caught hold of him. That's how close...he came to dying that day."

Calling a strict disciplinarian like Morris a liar only begged for a severe response. "I knew the Colonel would never stand being called a liar," Wightman said. "He sentenced him to seven days in the dungeon with nothing but bread and water." According to Wightman, "The only thing like a dungeon were the ovens in the old Malleable Iron Factory, which were great big monstrous caverns where they would put iron in with great big ponderous doors on them." In addition to a loaf of bread and some water "he was issued a pair of blankets...and there he was."

But Trotsky's time in the "dungeon" only lasted two days.

A group of about five hundred and thirty German prisoners, who had spent a month being schooled by Comrade Trotsky, now came to his aid. They protested his incarceration and silencing with a petition. Trotsky said, "A plebiscite like this, carried out in the very face of [the guards'] heavy-handed supervision was more than ample compensation for all the hardships of the Amherst imprisonment."

TORNIO, FINLAND

After five days of travel aboard a sealed train, Vladimir Ilyich Ulyanov, his wife, and several other revolutionaries descended upon the Swedish border town of Haparanda. Ulyanov—or as he is more commonly known, Vladimir Lenin—was travelling (according to Winston Churchill) "like a plague bacillus from Switzerland to Russia."

Without the German train and German money, Lenin could not have achieved revolution. The amount of German money involved was not insignificant. Close to fifty million marks (two hundred million dollars in today's values) was earmarked to ensure that the Bolsheviks would remove the Russian army from the war. Without Lenin, the Germans would not have created a one-front war, thus freeing one million men to fight on the western front. Without the British, Trotsky would not have been in place to try to prevent that one-front war at Brest-Litovsk; without the Germans, he could not have furthered the revolution with his one-time friend Lenin.

As Lenin's train pulled in to Haparanda, Sweden on Saturday, 15 April 1917, he sensed trouble. He assembled his group on the train and instructed them that, should they be arrested at the border, they were to insist that it was their right as Russians to return to their homeland now that the Czar was gone. Lenin knew that the orders of the provisional government allowing all exiled ex-patriates back into the country may not extend to him and his party.

Tornio, Finland was the opposing border town across the Torniojoki River. Because its Swedish counterpart was snowbound, Lenin's group was forced to travel across the river in horse-drawn sledges.

Grigory Zinoviev, Lenin's aide-de-camp in Switzerland for three years, said,

> "I remember that it was night. There was a long ribbon of sledges. On each sledge there were two people. Tension as they approached the Finnish border reached its maximum. The most uninhibited of the young people—Ussievich—was unusually taut. Vladimir Ilyich was outwardly calm. He was most of all interested in what was happening in far-off Petersburg…Across the frozen bay with its deep snowdrifts…fifteen hundred versts ahead…"

When they reached the Finnish border, it was not the Russian soldiers that were the problem. It was the British officers that posed the greatest obstacle to their progress.

During the war, the British Secret Intelligence Service, under the control of Mansfield Cumming—or "C," as he was more commonly referred to as—had a system of spies throughout Russia, increasingly as it became more apparent that Russia was descending into an even darker chaos.

As with Captain Makins in Halifax, Harry Gruner was working as British military control officer in one of the outer reaches of the war, in his case the border between Sweden and Finland. Gruner immediately noted the nervousness of the group. More importantly, though, he recognized Lenin. He knew the prize he had before him, but he was unsure how to keep him from entering Russia. Britain had been following Lenin`s progress from the time he left Switzerland. There was no way to keep him from returning home because the provisional government had decreed that all exiled political refugees could return—bar none.

Despite the edict, Gruner decided to telegraph the provisional government. He explained who he had at Tornio and asked whether he should allow him and his party to proceed. While he awaited a reply, he began to interrogate the Russians before him.

Mikhail Tskhakaya, a fellow revolutionary from exile in Geneva, said about the interrogation, "We were undressed to the skin. My son and I were forced to take off our stockings. I don't know what they were looking for. All the documents and even the children's books and toys my son had brought with him were taken."

Lenin was also heavily scrutinized. All manner of question was asked of him, and his luggage was thoroughly checked. He remained unflappable, calm and collected, firm in the knowledge that he was well within his right to be entering the country of his birth.

According to Tskhakaya, Lenin "observed the officers were disappointed at having found nothing." He continued, "Ilyich broke into happy laughter and, embracing me, he said 'Our trials, Comrade Mikha, have ended. We're on native land and we'll show them'—and he clenched his fist—'that we are worthy masters of the future.'"

By late on Sunday evening, 16 April 1917, Gruner received word from the provisional government, reminding him that "the new

Russian Government rested on a democratic foundation. Lenin's group should be allowed to enter." And with that order, he stamped their documents and ushered him and his fellow Russian revolutionaries into the country.

In later years, Gruner was mercilessly teased and derided for allowing Lenin to get away. His fellow soldiers accused him of "locking the stable door when the horse was out, or, rather, in." Others told him that he was quite fortunate not to be Japanese, or else "he would have to commit hara-kiri."

Unfortunately for Gruner, by the end of 1917, he was arrested and sentenced to death by Lenin himself for the treatment accorded him and his party at the Finnish border in 1917. The order was never carried out.

For a short period of a day and one half, British Secret Intelligence Service had held within its grasp the two main players of the Bolshevik revolution. Had Gruner informed Cumming as well, or had that officer run Trotsky through with his bayonet in Amherst, Nova Scotia, the outcome of the twentieth century may well have been different.

NATALYA SEDOVA

While Trotsky was otherwise disposed in Amherst, his wife, Natalya Sedova, and two sons remained in Halifax under the watchful eyes of the authorities. Trotsky said, "Notwithstanding the fact that my wife was never a political emigrant, that she left Russia upon a legal passport, that she has never appeared abroad upon the political arena, she was also arrested with my two boys, eleven and nine years of age respectively." He said that he used the word "arresting" intentionally and that it "is not merely a figure of speech."

He lamented the fact that the British wanted to separate his children from their mother but that she would not allow the authorities to place them "in an asylum." Instead, the remaining three members of Trotsky's family were housed with an Anglo-Russian police officer, David Horowetz, "who, fearing the 'illegal' sending of letters or telegrams, would not let the children out on the street, even without their mother, except under a strict watch."

Due to wartime restrictions, little was known at the time of Trotsky's detention in Amherst. Only after the November revolution, when Lenin, Trotsky, and the rest of the Bolsheviks seized power in Russia, did news begin to trickle out and the affair began to be reported on.

An article entitled *"Russian Revolutionist Trotsky and Family Were in N.S. for Several Weeks"* appeared in *The Halifax Herald*. It described Natalya Sedova as being "plentifully supplied with money and the day she was detained she requested that she be allowed to go to a hotel where she was prepared to pay ten dollars a day." That was a princely sum in 1917, and it seems highly doubtful that the British would allow her to keep any funds once "arrested" and removed from the *S.S. Kristianiafjord*.

In the same issue, *The Halifax Herald* described Ms. Sedova as:

> "A petite brown-haired woman of about thirty-six years of age…While at the Horowitz home she was bitter in denunciation of the way in which she was being guarded. She insisted that she and her husband had committed no crime and that they were victims of the Czar's agents through the American and British Governments. She told Mr. Horowitz that she and her husband had left Paris for New York so as to get a steamer to Bergen and in that reach St. Petersburg. They believed that they would be welcome in the United States and Canada, but they found that the Czar's influence was too far reaching."

Trotsky, forever the outraged revolutionary, wrote in his memoirs:

> "At first the Canadian authorities tried to separate [the children] from their mother and put them in a children's

home. Overwhelmed by such a prospect, my wife declared that she would never allow them to separate her from her boys. And it was only because of her protest that the boys were placed with her in the house of an Anglo-Russian police agent. To prevent 'illegal' despatch of letters and telegrams, this functionary allowed the children to go out only with an escort, even when they were not with their mother. It was not until eleven days later that my wife and the children were allowed to move to a hotel, on condition that they report each day at the police station."

Natalya quickly began to dislike staying at the Horowetz home. She described the abode as "utter squalor" and her host as "so stupid as to be comical. Having been ordered to keep a discreet watch over me, he nevertheless boasted to me of his many disguises."

However, by mid-April, she and the children moved to the Prince George Hotel on Sackville and Hollis Streets, where they remained until their departure for Europe later in the month. On one occasion, though, Mrs. Trotsky was overheard proclaiming, "If I ever get back to my own country, I will talk, I will write, I will let my country people know that Canada is not free, that the United States is not free, that there is as much slavery in these countries as there is in Siberia." If she did not keep to her word, her husband most assuredly did.

Natalya and the children found living in Halifax on their own a difficult prospect. With no friends and a small Russian population in the area to draw upon for support, and by virtue of the fact that they were unable to speak English, day-to-day living was a daunting endeavour.

Natalya befriended Fanny Horowetz, the adult daughter of her one-time host. Fanny spoke Russian and recalled seeing Natalya struggle with English. One day, while shopping for a notepad on Barrington Street, Fanny witnessed Natalya's revolutionary nature. The store clerk showed Natalya a pad embellished with the flags of all the Allied nations. She immediately stated in Russian, "I want none of them...I have no use for any flags but the flag of real freedom."

She was referring to the red flag.

PRESSURE INCREASES

By mid-April, pressure began to mount on the Canadian government to do something about the Trotsky issue. On 15 April 1917, Louis Fraina, an Italian-born American socialist who had befriended Trotsky during his brief stay in New York, organized a "revolutionary socialist" gathering in Manhattan to protest Trotsky's incarceration in Canada and the war. Even though he would help to create the United States Communist Party in 1919, he was under a constant cloud of suspicion of being both an American and a British spy.

In addition to the Fraina gathering, the "Russian Colony of Pittsburg" also sent a telegram to the British Embassy in Washington, protesting the "suppressing over the citizens of Russia and request[ing]...their immediate release." There was also the letter sent by Aleinikoff, as well as a couple other missives, to various members of the Canadian government and military. In Russia, the revolutionary newspaper *Pravda* also agitated for

Trotsky's release and made life uncomfortable for the provisional government.

In a surprising note to the naval secretary of the Interdepartmental Committee (an oversight committee made up of military, naval, and senior civil servants who normally rubber-stamped the head of Canada's Militia and Defence's requests), Maj-General Gwatkin wrote of Trotsky's case. He said, "An act of high-handed injustice had been done."

On 16 April, Admiral C.E. Kingsmill, Director of the Canadian Naval Service, asked Captain Makins to correspond with his superiors at the Admiralty in London about finding an expeditious end to this unfortunate saga. Was the Canadian government and/or military receiving a large amount of distress over the internment of Trotsky and the others? And if so, where exactly was this pressure coming from: friend or foe?

Makins agreed to send a note to the admiral, but on 20 April 1917, he sent a note to Kingsmill highlighting the rally in New York City on the fifteenth, which carried a large German contingent of socialists. Because of this incident, he argued, internment was warranted and in the best interests of the British.

On 16 April, the Russian Charge d'Affaires in Montreal sent a memo to the British Foreign Office in London, inquiring as to the current disposition of the internees in Nova Scotia. He reminded them that Trotsky and the others held proper and lawful Russian passports and that these were acceptable under the terms of the Russian general amnesty. It seemed odd that Lenin was only held for a day and a half using this point, and Trotsky, even after an official of the provisional government in Montreal pointed this out, was held in a Canadian jail for a month in total. Obviously, there was more at play than mere money. Lenin had fifty million marks, and at best, Trotsky had ten thousand U.S. dollars. Lenin virtually rode through Torvio, and Trotsky spent a month in Amherst Nova Scotia. Something was amiss.

Another odd happenstance was the arrival of MI5 officer Claude Dansey in Halifax. He was the senior British MI5 officer responsible for port intelligence; he decided who could enter or leave a British territory. Dansey was one of Britain's most senior intelligence officials. With nearly thirty years of service, he had learned his spy craft in Rhodesia in the 1890s and practised it during the Boer War. For three years prior to 1914, he spied on Irish nationalists and U.S. bankers in America. Code name "Z," he was one of the initial agents for Britain's Secret Service Bureau [forerunner of MI5 and MI6] when it was first constructed in 1909.

Dansey had been travelling with the British Foreign Secretary, Arthur Balfour. Dansey had been scheduled to arrive in America in mid-April, where he was slated to replace William Wiseman as head of intelligence operations in America (a post he ultimately never assumed for some unknown reason). He arrived during the first week of April instead.

Dansey was aware of the Trotsky arrest before arriving in Halifax. He immediately smelled a rat. He telegraphed Wiseman for information on Trotsky as soon as he arrived. Wiseman did not reply.

Dansey also sought out Captain Makins to get his side of the affair. "I believed the new Russian government would at once ask for Trotsky's release," he told Makins during their meeting. "Unless [the British naval authorities] were very certain of the source of the information against him, it would be much better to let him go before he got angry." Makins assured Dansey that he would contact New York and Washington and "ascertain the reliability of their information."

By the time he reached New York via Halifax, he seemed

convinced that holding Trotsky was not warranted. It is probable that while in Halifax, Dansey would have availed himself of the close proximity to visit and question the fiery Russian revolutionary only ninety miles up the rail line. It is almost certain that Foreign Secretary Balfour knew who Trotsky was and of his value. At the same time, the British were monitoring Lenin's progress across Scandinavia as he moved towards Russia. Dansey, giving his added stamp to allowing Trotsky to proceed, gives added weight to the British having "turned" Trotsky.

The naval attaché at the British Embassy in Washington, Guy Gaunt, did his level best at every turn to stymy Wiseman's career. It would have taken a superior at MI5, like Claude Dansey, to keep a reign on him. All the pieces were moving into place.

Whether Trotsky had cold feet, or they were simply cementing his cover, we may never know for sure. One thing is certain, though: the British needed Trotsky to keep Russia in the war. Trotsky needed British money. He needed to spread the revolution simultaneously across Europe and the world, and he could not do that by signing a separate peace. If Lenin was destroyed during the process, then so much the better. Lenin had the Germans. Trotsky had the British. Even in 1917, a sort of "cold war" atmosphere began to percolate.

Trotsky continued to ruminate publicly about why he and the others were interned. He already knew. He complained to the provisional government, asking, "Who arrested us, and on what grounds? That the general order to detain those Russian citizens who happened to hold views not acceptable to the British government really emanated from the British government is without any doubt, for Mr. Lloyd George could not miss the happily offered opportunity to reveal, at last, that titanic energy, in the name of which he came to power."

Trotsky could have been working with the British, so he would know the answer to this. He may have needed a cover story to give him a bit of street credibility when back in Russia.

Trotsky continued:

> "There is one more question, namely, who pointed us out to the British-Canadian authorities as persons who should be detained? Who furnished Halifax in the short space of three or four days the information as to our views? A line of circumstances points to the fact that this allied service was rendered by the renovated Russian consulate, the same consulate which had removed Nicholas' portrait from its reception room and has stricken the word 'Imperial' from its title.
>
> "Handing out to us with one hand the papers entitling us to a safe conduct to Russia and demonstrating thereby its loyalty towards the amnesty which to them appeared so unreliable, the consulate could with its other hand furnish its secret information to the British authorities, hoping that its activity in this direction would prove to be at any rate more reliable."

Relief for all concerned arrived on 20 April, when the admiral declared that the "Russian socialists should be allowed to proceed." This was the day after Dansey met with Captain Makins. No other reason was given. No other reason was needed.

Makins delivered the news to Ottawa that he was instructed to make the earliest possible provisions for the earliest possible departure of the Russians. Gwatkin, the Canadian military chief of staff, told Postmaster General Coulter, "Our friends the Russian socialists are to be released. Arrangements are being made for their passage to Europe."

Even with the order being given to release the Russians, the British authorities took their time in giving the order to spring them from captivity. One Foreign Office bureaucrat said, "We must permit but need not expedite their journey."

On 27 April 1917, Makins informed Canadian authorities that, "Arrangements have been made to send the Russian Socialists now interned at Amherst to Russia by the Danish ship *S.S. Hellig Olav*. They will embark on Sunday morning, the 29th April."

The day of Trotsky's departure from Amherst was as eventful as his entry into Canada. Trotsky described the day in his usual vitriolic and forceful way:

> "We were ordered to pack our things and proceed under convoy. When we demanded the why and wherefore, they refused to say anything. The prisoners became excited because they thought we were being taken to a fortress. We asked for the nearest Russian Consul; they refused us again. We had reason enough for not trusting these highwaymen of the sea, and so we insisted that we would not go voluntarily until they told us where we were going. The commander ordered forcible measures. Soldiers of the convoy carried out our luggage, but we stayed stubbornly in our bunks. It was only when the convoy was faced with the task of carrying us out bodily just as we had been taken off a steamer a month earlier, and of doing it in the midst of a crowd of excited sailors, that the commander relented and told us, in his characteristic Anglo-Colonial way, that we were to sail on a Danish boat for Russia. The colonel's purple face twitched convulsively. He could not bear the thought that we were escaping him."

Trotsky cheekily took one final stab at Morris by lamenting for him: "If it had been on the African coast!" Morris, for sure, would have been happy just to see Trotsky leave his otherwise peaceful camp.

The revolutionary continued triumphantly:

> "As we were being taken away from the camp, our fellow prisoners gave us a most impressive send-off. Although the officers shut themselves up in their compartment, and only a few poked their noses through the chinks, the sailors and workers lined the passages on both sides, an improvised band played the revolutionary march ['The Internationale'], and friendly hands were extended to us from every quarter. One of the prisoners delivered a short speech acclaiming the Russian revolution and cursing the German monarchy. Even now it makes me happy to remember that in the very midst of the war, we were fraternizing with German sailors in Amherst...."

"An improvised band" at the Amherst Internment Camp, World War I. (Author's Collection)

Yet the possibility exists that not all members of Trotsky's party left for Halifax that same day. The internment camp's war diary for that week indicates that only five men were "taken to Halifax under escort to be placed on steamer bound for Petrograd." Left off the list was Konstantin Romanchenko, the thirty-two-year-old carpenter whose past is as ambiguous as his life after Amherst was. Had he been a British or and Okhrana plant in Trotsky's little cabal? The Okhrana were exemplary at embedding agents into the ranks and cells of revolutionaries intent on fomenting unrest in the motherland. Is that why former Russian Ambassador to the United States Andrei Kalpaschnikoff was aboard the *S.S. Kristianiafjord*? Was he there to keep an eye on his assets?

Accusations were made starting in late March 1917 that Leon Trotsky was himself an Okhrana agent, beginning in 1902. A report on 30 March from the Quartermaster-General of the Imperial Army Staff Headquarters, addressed to the provisional government, stated that "a military agent in the U.S.A. had cabled that Trotsky had sailed from New York on the *S.S. Christianiafjord* (sic)...and that, according to British intelligence, Trotsky was in charge of peace propaganda in America, paid by the Germans and by persons sympathetic to them."

The military agent most likely had to have been Kalpaschnikoff, who was indeed working in concert with Wiseman, as British and Russian interests aligned. By this time, the Political Investigating Committee created by the Kerensky Provisional Government alleged that "even...Leon Trotsky had served in the Okhrana as a special agent."

The extent and the scope of Trotsky's involvement with the Okhrana may never be fully known. By 1938, Stalin had completed his Moscow show trials, and Trotsky was found guilty, along with other Bolsheviks, of conspiring to have Stalin murdered. During the exercise to expunge Trotsky from Soviet memory, the evidence of Trotsky's involvement with the Okhrana was brought to Stalin, and he immediately quashed this most damaging information. Why? Because Stalin had been involved with the Okhrana to a large extent from the early part of the century, right up into and immediately after the October Revolution. To use this information against Trotsky would risk exposing his own involvement with the Okhrana, and since he really did not need a whole lot of truth to purge the memory of Trotsky from Russian history, it was more important to protect his involvement with the Czar's secret police.

One of Trotsky's party seemed to disappear after they left Amherst; his affiliations were unknown. Former Russian Ambassador to the United States Andrei Kalpaschnikoff was either keeping an eye on Trotsky, in league with the British but taking his orders from the Okhrana, or he was working in league with Trotsky as Okhrana agents. Trotsky, by all accounts, was taking money from the Germans, the British, Germanic-American Jewish financier Jacob Schiff, or the American government. Upon his return to Russia and after the October Revolution Trotsky assumed the portfolio as Foreign Minister, and promptly had Kalpaschnikoff imprisoned.

In 1919, a compatriot of Trotsky during his early Okhrana days, a man named Khrustulev-Nosar, wrote a tell-all book about the former's involvement with the Czar's secret police. "On Trotsky's direct orders, with the aim of removing this witness to his collaboration with the Okhrana," Khrustulev-Nosar was executed later in 1919 at Trotsky's command. It seemed Trotsky was trying to eliminate any evidence of his duplicity with the one thing which could truly ruin his reputation and his life—co-operation with the Czar. It seems that Trotsky's pragmatism (or more aptly, prostitution) really did know no bounds.

Leon Trotsky arriving in Petrograd by train on May 4 1917. (Wikimedia Commons)

Trotsky and company were taken by train back to Halifax one final time to meet up with Trotsky's family and Captain Makins. Of that meeting, Trotsky wrote:

> "Machen (sic), the British police officer who had brought about our arrest, was present at our departure. As a parting shot I warned him that my first business in the Constituent Assembly would be to question foreign minister Miliukov about the outrageous treatment of Russian citizens by the Anglo-Canadian police. 'I hope,' said Machen (sic) in quick retort, 'that you will never get into the Constituent Assembly.'"

The British, of course, had a desperate need to keep the Russian army in the field. The war had not been going as planned. Admittedly, the Americans had just recently declared war on Germany, but it would take months to get American soldiers on the ground in Europe. Sir William Wiseman, New York Bureau chief of MI1(c) was determined to "guide the storm" in Russia. The revolution may not have been able to be stopped, but parts of it could be managed, especially Germany's influence in Russia.

Counter to Lenin's betrayal for the call of the defeat of the Russian nation to the Germans, Trotsky cheered the prospect of war as a means to the revolution that by no means meant being fatalistic. Trotsky hoped that his Russian revolution would simultaneously spread throughout Europe. He had to balance those hopes between Lenin's, whose idea it was to secure the Russian portion of the revolution first; and between the communists who hoped for a pan-European revolutionary war that would lead to a Soviet-style republic encompassing all of Europe.

His balancing act failed. Lenin seized the day, and despite his wish to set Europe ablaze in a revolutionary maelstrom, those who hitched their horse to Trotsky's cart were sorely disappointed. Russia would leave the war.

All the parties involved in the Trotsky affair were happy to see him go, albeit for different reasons. The Canadian government did not need the headaches. The British needed Russia to be kept in the war at all costs. The Russian provisional government were glad to ease the pressure for the continued incarceration of Trotsky and his fellow revolutionaries.

Colonel Morris, the beleaguered jailer in Amherst, in a letter to his superior, wrote, "Of course I am aware that the opinions of [Trotsky's party] may be of little or no importance, but Leon Trotsky, the leader is a man holding extremely strong views and of most powerful personality, his personality being such that after only a few days stay here was by far the most popular man in the camp with the German prisoners of war, two-thirds of whom are socialists."

The trip back to Europe was rocky for all aboard the S.S. *Hellig Olav*. Natalya recalled that they were "pounded mercilessly by the Atlantic waves." Trotsky recalled the voyage as boring and uneventful. The only upside to the trip was that Chudnovski fell in love with and "paid court to a little Russian dancer" he met on the ship, according to Natalya.

Trotsky was free to continue the struggle that he had begun so many years before. The British, the Canadians, and the Americans posed no further barrier to his plans and those of his fellow Russians who were long-suffering for change in Russia. Much lay ahead for Trotsky, but one thing was for sure: his time was now.

BIBLIOGRAPHY

MANUSCRIPT SOURCE
Dalhousie University Archives:

MS-2-306, SF Box 36, Folder 26 – Transcript of John Bell's interview with F.C. Wightman about Leon Trotsky's month at the Amherst Internment Camp during World War One. 1976.

National Archives of Canada:

"Arrests of Certain Russians on S.S. Kristiania, 1917." (RG25-A-3-a)

Otter Papers

Public Archives of Nova Scotia: Manuscript Group 100

NEWSPAPERS
Amherst Daily News
Globe and Mail
Halifax Chronicle Herald
Jewish Daily Forward
New York Call
New York Times
Novy Mir

BOOKS
Ackerman, Kenneth. *Trotsky in New York 1917: A Radical On The Eve of Revolution,* Berkely, Ca: Counterpoint, 2016.

Avery, Donald. *Dangerous Foreigners,* Toronto: McClelland and Stewart, 1979.

Buchanan, George. *My Mission to Moscow,* 2 volumes. London: Cassell and Company, 1923.

Cohen, Naomi W. *Jacob H. Schiff: A study in American Jewish Leadership.* Hanover, NH: University Press of New England, Brandeis University Press, 1999.

Crane, Charles. *Memoirs of Charles R. Crane.* Unpublished,1934.

Deutscher, Isaac. *The Prophet Armed: Trotsky, 1879-1921.* New York: Oxford University Press, 1954.

Eastman, Max. *The Young Trotsky.* London: New Park Publications, 1926, 1980.

Epstein, Edward Jay. *Dossier: The Secret History of Armand Hammer*. New York: Carroll and Graf, 1996

Gilbert, Martin. *Churchill and the Jews*. Toronto: McClelland and Stewart, 2008.

Goldman, Emma. *Living My Life*. New York: Da Capo Press, 1931, 1970.

Hapgood, David. Charles R. Crane: The Man who Bet on People. New York: Xlibris Corp, 2000.

Kalpaschnikoff, Andrew. *A Prisoner of Trotsky*. Garden City, NY: Doubleday, Page & Company, 1920.

Leblanc, Paul. *Trotsky*. London: Reaktion Books, 2015.

Lee, Albert. *Henry Ford and the Jews*. Briarcliff Manor, NY: Stein & Day, 1980.

Morton, Desmond. *The Canadian General: Sir William Otter*. Toronto: Hakkert, 1974.

Service, Robert. *Trotsky: A Biography*. London: Pan Books, 2010.

Spence, Richard. *Trust No One: The Secret World of Sidney Reilly*. Los Angeles: Feral House, 2002.

Steffens, Lincoln. *The Autobiography of Lincoln Steffens*. New York: Harcourt, Brace, 1931.

Sutton, Anthony. *Wall Street and the Bolshevik Revolution.* West Hoathly, UK: Clairview Books, 1974, 2011.

Thatcher, Ian. *Leon Trotsky and World War One: August 1914-February 1917.* New York: St. Martin's Press, 2000.

Thatcher, Ian. *Trotsky.* London: Routledge, Taylor & Francis Group, 2003.

Thwaites, Norman. G. *Velvet & Vinegar.* London: Grayson & Grayson, 1932.

Trotsky, Leon. *My Life: An Attempt at an Autobiography.* New York: Grossett and Dunlap, Inc,. 1930

Trotsky, Leon. *The Russian Revolution: The Overthrow of Tsarism and the Triumph of the Soviets.* New York: Doubleday Anchor Books, 1932, 1959.

Ultan, Lloyd. *The Beautiful Bronx, 1920-1950.* New York: Bronx County Historical Society, 1979.

Ultan, Lloyd, and Gary Hermalyn. *The Bronx in the Innocent Years, 1890-1925.* New York: Harper & Row, 1964, 1985.

ARTICLES

Bolton, K.R. "Responses of International Capital to the Russian Revolutions." *International Journal of Russian Studies*, no.1, 2012: 43-61.

Cameron, Silver Donald. "Trotsky in Amherst." *Canadian Geographic*, 1988.

Churchill, Winston S. "Zionism versus Bolshevism: A Struggle for the Soul of the Jewish People." *Illustrated Sunday Herald*, February 8, 1920.

Griffin, Frederick C. "Leon Trotsky in New York City." *New York History* 49, no. 4 (October 1968): 391-403.

Lore, Ludwig. "Leon Trotsky." *Class Struggle*, November 7, 1918.

Lore, Ludwig. "When Trotsky Lived in New York," Special Collections, Browne Manuscripts, Lilly Library, Indiana University.

MacLean, J.B. "Why Did We Let Trotsky Go? Canada Lost an Opportunity to Shorten the War." *MacLean's*, July 1919.

Morton, Desmond. "Sir William Otter and Internment Operations in Canada During the First World War." *Canadian Historical Review*, Vol LV (1974): 38-55.

Moskowitz, Henry. "Trotsky on the East Side." *Outlook*, January 30, 1918.

Pitzer, Andrea. "Trotsky's Canadian Holiday." *Lapham's Quarterly*, April 28, 2014.

Roberts, Priscilla. "Jewish Bankers, Russia, and the Soviet Union, 1900-1940: The Case of Kuhn, Loeb and Company," American Jewish Archives Journal 49, no. 1-2 (1997): 9-37.

Rodney, W. "Broken Journey: Trotsky in Canada,1917." *Queen's Quarterly*, Vol 74 (1967): 649-665.

Routsky, Pierre. "A Page From the Past," *Russian Review*, 7, no. 2 (Spring 1948): 69-75.

Schurer, Heinz. "Alexander Helphand-Parvus: Russian Revolutionary and German Patriot." *Russian Review* 18, no 4 (October 1959).

Shepherd, William G. "The Road To Red Russia." *Everybody's Magazine*, Vol 37, no.1 (July 1917): 1-12.

Spence, Richard. "Catching Louis Fraina: Loyal Communist, US Government Informant, or British Agent?" *American Communist History* 11, no 1 (2012).

Spence, Richard. "Hidden Agendas: Spies, Lies, and Intrigue Surrounding Trotsky's American Visit of January-April 1917." *Revolutionary Russia* 21, no. 1 (June 2008): 33-55.

Spence, Richard. "Interrupted Journey: British Intelligence and the arrest of Leon Trotskii, April 1917," *Revolutionary Russia* 13, no.1 (June 2000): 1-28.

Spence, Richard. "The Tsar's Other Lietenant: The Antisemitic Activities of Boris L'vovich Brazol, 1919-1960." Part 1, "Beilis, the Protocols, and Henry Ford," *Journal for the Study of Antisemitism* 4, no. 1 (2012): 199-220.

Thatcher, Ian. "Leon Trotsky in New York City." *Historical Research* 69, no.169 (June 1966): 166.

Trotsky, Leon. "In British Captivity, 1917." *Class Struggle* 2, no.4 (December 1918).

Trotsky, Leon. "The Life Story of Trotsky." *The Observer*, (September 1929), n.p.

Truro, Aaron Beswick. "Leon Trotsky Forged Notable Month at Amherst Foundry-Turned Internment Camp." *Chronicle Herald* (Halifax), January 2, 2015.

Ultan, Lloyd. "The Mystery of Trotsky's Bronx Friend." Bronx County Historical Society Journal 36, no. 2 (Fall 1999): 73.

Werner, H. "And What, Exactly was Leon Trotsky Doing in Nova Scotia in 1917?" Saturday Night, (August 1974): 26-29.

www.ingramcontent.com/pod-product-compliance
Lightning Source LLC
Chambersburg PA
CBHW070431010526
44118CB00014B/1999